Professor Barclay was a distinguished scholar, an exceptionally gifted preacher and a regular broadcaster. His writings for the *British Weekly* were very popular and for twenty years from 1950 a full page every week was given to them. From 1963 until 1974 he was Professor of Divinity and Biblical Criticism at Glasgow University. He was a Member of the Advisory Committee working on the New English Bible and also a Member of the Apocrypha Panel of Translators. In 1975 he was appointed a Visiting Professor at the University of Strathclyde for a period of three years where he lectured on Ethics, and in the same year—jointly with the Rev. Professor James Stewart—he received the 1975 Citation from the American theological organization The Upper Room; the first time it has been awarded outside America. His extremely popular *Bible Study Notes* using his own translation of the New Testament have achieved a world-wide sale.

Professor Barclay died in January 1978.

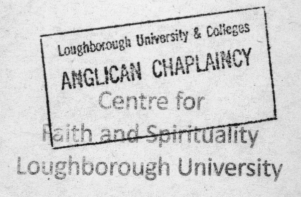

WILLIAM BARCLAY

# *More Prayers for Young People*

## Collins

FOUNT PAPERBACKS

William Collins Sons & Cod. Ltd
London · Glasgow · Sydney · Auckland
Toronto · Johannesburg

First published in Great Britain in 1977 by Fount
Paperbacks
Seventh impression November 1990

Fount Paperbacks is an imprint of
Collins Religious Division,
part of the Collins Publishing Group
8 Grafton Street, London W1X 3LA

Printed and bound in Great Britain by William Collins
Sons & Co. Ltd, Glasgow

# CONTENTS

Foreword     6

On Praying     7

Prayers with Bible Readings for Forty-Two Days     12

Prayers for Special Occasions     96

# FOREWORD

I should be sadly lacking in courtesy if I did not express my thanks to those who have helped in the writing of this book.

First of all, I wish to thank Lady Collins who in the first instance suggested the book and then waited with patience for it. Secondly, I wish to thank my secretary, Mrs D. Hamilton, who typed it and whose advice was always helpful.

As to the book itself, each day's contents begin with a prayer written for the occasion, and then a scripture reading, and finally there is a prayer written by someone famous in history or in literature. The Bible readings over the six weeks are designed to form a life of Christ.

It is my hope and prayer that this book may be of some use to young people. It is only designed to be a beginning and the aim of the book will be realized if the time comes when those who use it can throw it away and make their own prayers to God.

*Glasgow, June 1976*                               WILLIAM BARCLAY

# ON PRAYING

The great men said their prayers themselves and encouraged others to do so. Charles Dickens wrote the following letter to his youngest son who went out to Australia in 1868:

'I need not tell you that I love you dearly and am very, very sorry in my heart to part with you. I have put a New Testament among your books because it is the best book that ever was, or will be, known in the world. As your brothers have gone away one by one I have written to each such words as I am now writing to you, entreating them all to guide themselves by this book. Only one thing more, never abandon the practice of private prayer. I know the comfort of it.'

So Dickens writes to his son never to abandon the practice of private prayer. Aldous Huxley was one of the greatest of the moderns and in the second volume of his biography by Sybille Bedford, it is said of him that he was asked once, 'Aldous, do you pray?' He answered: 'I always say my prayers – in the simplest possible words, I always begin "Now I lay me down to sleep" – and my prayers are nearly always answered.' So then, the great men in every generation have said their prayers, and this is what this book is designed to help you to do.

The first question we ask about our prayers is 'What shall I say?' This book is designed to tell you what to say, but it is also meant to make you able to speak for yourself, and its aim will be realized if the day comes when you throw it away and need it no longer. In prayer we can say anything we like to God because we can talk to him in the simplest and most straightforward manner.

Another question that we must ask is 'How will I keep my thoughts from wandering?' It is very difficult to think of any subject for any length of time. In fact, it has been said that it is impossible to think of the one thing, and nothing but the one thing, for even as short a time as two minutes. When we pray we find this, that and the next thought coming into our minds. Frank Boreham tells how C. Aubrey Price gave him a bit of good advice, and this was 'Always pray *aloud*'. It is much easier to concentrate when we are actually speaking aloud than when we are merely speaking into ourselves.

It will help to concentrate our thoughts if we pray in an orderly way. There are five different kinds of prayer:

The prayer of approach;
the prayer of confession;
the prayer of thanksgiving;
the prayer of petition;
the prayer of intercession.

In the prayer of approach we make ourselves aware of the presence of God around us and about us. In the prayer of confession we ask God's forgiveness for the wrong things that we have done. In the prayer of thanksgiving we give thanks for the many gifts with which we are surrounded. In the prayer of petition we bring our own special needs and desires to God. In the prayer of intercession we pray for other people.

The next question we ask is 'What can I expect when I pray?' When we pray we ought to be quite sure what we are doing. Very often we pray to God to save us from something or to take something away from us. The real prayer is not so much to ask God to be saved from things. The real prayer is for help to conquer whatever situation we are in – not to be liberated from the thing, but to overcome it.

The next question we might ask is 'When do I pray?' Ideally, the best time to pray is night and morning, but it is possible to pray anywhere. Sir Thomas Browne, the famous physician, says:

'I have resolved to pray more and to pray always, to pray in all places where quietness inviteth, in the house, on the highway, in the streets; and to know no street or passage in this city that may not witness that I have not forgotten God.'

8

Sir Thomas Browne meant that even going about his daily business he could pray anywhere, and so can we.

The next question we may well ask is 'What must be my physical attitude in prayer?' We must not think there is any one answer to this question. The only answer which is valid for everyone is that we ought to pray in a position in which our body is comfortable, because if we do not some slight discomfort will interfere with our concentration, and we will think more of the discomfort than of the prayer.

Another mistake that we make regularly is that we think too much of prayer in the sense of us talking to God. In prayer there should be just as much of listening to God. Prayer is not a monologue, it is a dialogue. Brother Lawrence said that his aim was 'that we should establish ourselves in a sense of God's presence by continual conversing with him', and conversation with anyone demands silence as well as speaking. We have therefore in prayer not only to talk to God but to listen to God.

It will be of the greatest possible help to prayer if we succeed in living a life in which we are always conscious of God; not just conscious of him in the crisis or the emergency, but conscious of him always. Someone has put it this way. 'The commandment says "Remember the Sabbath Day, to keep it holy", but we ought to say "Remember the week day, to keep it holy".' Every day is a day when we ought to pray, and every place is a place where we ought to pray, and it comes most easily when, wherever we are, we are aware of the presence of God.

I hope you will find this book useful, but I would also hope, as I have already said, that you will soon arrive at a stage when you don't need it, when you can make your own prayers and when you can put this book away, having finished with its usefulness.

*More Prayers for Young People*

Help me, O God, to go out to begin this week's work in your company.

Help me to remember that you are always with me, and so help me to make everything I do and everything I say fit for you to see and to hear.

Help me never to do or to say anything which would bring sorrow to those who live with me, grief to you, or shame to myself; through Jesus Christ my Lord. Amen.

### THE BIRTH OF JESUS

This was the way in which the birth of Jesus took place. Mary his mother was pledged to be married to Joseph, but, before they became man and wife, it was discovered that she was going to have a child, as a result of the action of the Holy Spirit. Although Joseph, her intended husband, was a man who strictly kept the Law, he had no desire publicly to humiliate her, so he wished to divorce her secretly. While he was planning to do this, an angel of the Lord appeared to him in a dream. 'Joseph, son of David,' the angel said, 'do not hesitate to marry Mary, for it is as a result of the action of the Holy Spirit that she is going to have a child. She will have a son, and you must call him by the name Jesus, for it is he who will save his people from their sins.' All this happened that the statement made by the Lord through the prophet might come true:

'The virgin shall conceive and have a child, and they shall give him the name Emmanuel,'

for that name means, 'God is with us.' So Joseph woke from sleep and carried out the instructions of the angel of the Lord. He married Mary, but he did not have any inter-

course with her, until she had had her son. And he called
him by the name Jesus.

Matthew 1:18–25

O God who hast ordained that whatever is to be desired,
should be sought by labour, and who, by thy blessing,
bringest honest labour to good effect; look with mercy
upon my studies and endeavours. Grant me, O Lord, to
design only what is lawful and right; and afford me calm-
ness of mind and steadiness of purpose, that I may so do thy
will in this short life, as to obtain happiness in the world to
come, for the sake of Jesus Christ our Lord.

SAMUEL JOHNSON

Help me, O God, like Jesus to be growing all the time.

Help me to live in such a way that I will always bring health to my body, so that I may grow stronger and fitter every day.

Help me in my studies to widen and deepen my mind by learning some new thing each day, so that I may come to think for myself and to think wisely and to think well.

Help me to live in such a way that I may bring pleasure to those who love me, joy to you, and credit to myself; through Jesus Christ my Lord. Amen.

## THE BOY JESUS

Every year Jesus' parents used to go to Jerusalem for the Festival of the Passover. When he was twelve years old, they went up to the festival as they usually did. They stayed to the very end of the festival, and, when they were on their way back home, the boy Jesus stayed on in Jerusalem. His parents were not aware that he had done so. They thought that he was in the caravan, and, at the end of the first day's journey, they began to search for him among their relations and friends. When they did not find him, they turned back to Jerusalem, searching for him as they went. It was three days before they discovered him in the Temple precincts, sitting in the middle of the teachers, listening to them, and asking them questions. All the listeners were amazed at his intelligence and at his answers. They were very surprised to see him there. 'Child,' his mother said to him, 'why have you behaved like this to us? Your father and I have been searching for you, and we have been worried to distraction.' 'Why had you to look for me?' he said. 'Didn't you know that I was bound to be in my Father's house?'

They did not understand the meaning of what he said. So

he went down with them, and came to Nazareth, and he
was obedient to them. His mother stored all these things in
her memory and kept thinking about them. And Jesus grew
wiser in mind and bigger in body, and more and more he
won the approval of God and of his fellow men.

Luke 2:41–52

O Holy Spirit of God,
   who with thy holy breath doth cleanse the hearts and
     minds of men,
   comforting them when they be in sorrow,
   leading them when they be out of the way,
   kindling them when they be cold,
   knitting them together when they be at variance,
   and enriching them with manifold gifts;
     by whose working all things live:
We beseech thee to maintain and daily to increase the gifts
   which thou hast vouchsafed to us;
   that with thy light before us and within us we may pass
   through this world
     without stumbling and without straying;
   who livest and reignest with the Father and the Son,
   everlastingly.

ERASMUS

O God, bless me in every part of my life.
At home,
   help me to be thoughtful, considerate and kind.
At school,
   help me to be diligent, attentive and respectful to those
   who are in authority.
On the playing-field,
   help me to play hard, but to play fair. Help me not to
   boast if I win, and not to make excuses if I lose.
On the streets,
   help me never to behave in any way which would dis-
   honour the uniform I wear.
Make me at all times true to myself, true to my loved ones
   and true to you; through Jesus Christ my Lord. Amen.

### THE HOUR STRIKES

When the people were in a state of expectancy, and when
they were all debating in their minds whether John could
be the Messiah, John said to them all: 'I baptize you with
water, but the One who is stronger than I is coming. I am
not fit to untie the strap of his sandals. He will baptize you
with the Holy Spirit and with fire. He is going to winnow
the chaff from the corn. He will cleanse every speck of
rubbish from his threshing-floor, and gather the corn into
his granary, but he will burn the chaff with the fire that
nothing can put out.'

So, then, appealing to the people with these and many
another plea, John announced the Good News to them. But,
when Herod the tetrarch was reproved by him for his conduct in the matter of Herodias, his brother's wife, and for all
the other wicked things he had done, in addition to all his
other crimes, he shut up John in prison.

When all the people had been baptized, Jesus too was baptized, and, while he was praying, heaven was opened, and the Holy Spirit in bodily form came down like a dove on him, and there came a voice from heaven: 'You are my Son, the Beloved and Only One, on whom my favour rests.'

Luke 3:15–22

God be in my head
And in my understanding.
God be in mine eyes
And in my looking.
God be in my mouth
And in my speaking.
God be in my heart
And in my thinking.
God be at mine end
And at my departing.

SARUM PRIMER 1527

O God, when I am tempted, help me to resist temptation.

Make me resolved that I will never give those who love
me reason to blush for anything I have done.

Make me resolved never to do anything which would
lower my own self-respect.

Help me to remember that you are always there to give
me your help in the struggle.

Help me to live all through today in such a way that I
will have no regrets when evening comes; through
Jesus Christ my Lord. Amen.

## JESUS AND JOHN

John's coat was made of camel's hair, and he wore a leather
belt round his waist. His food consisted of locusts and wild
honey. People from Jerusalem and from all over Judaea and
from all over the Jordan valley flocked out to him. And a
continuous stream of them were baptized in the River
Jordan, while they confessed their sins.

When John saw the Pharisees and Sadducees coming in
large numbers to be baptized, he said to them: 'Brood of
vipers! Who put it into your heads to flee from the coming
wrath? Prove the sincerity of your repentance by your life
and conduct. Don't get the idea that you can say to yourselves: "We have Abraham as our father." For I tell you,
God can produce children for Abraham from these stones.
Even now the axe is poised at the root of the trees. Every
tree which does not produce good fruit is going to be cut
down and flung into the fire. I baptize you with water to
make you repent. He who is coming after me is stronger
than I am. I am not fit to carry his sandals. He will baptize
you with the Holy Spirit and with fire. He is going to
winnow the chaff from the corn, and he will clear every

speck of rubbish from his threshing-floor. His corn he will gather into the store-house; the chaff he will burn with fire that nothing can put out.'

At that time Jesus came from Galilee to the Jordan to be baptized by John. John tried to stop him. 'I need to be baptized by you,' he said, 'and are you coming to me?' 'For the present,' Jesus answered, 'let it be so, for the right thing for us to do is to do everything a good man ought to do.' Then John let him have his way. No sooner had Jesus been baptized and come out of the water, than the heavens were opened, and John saw the Spirit coming down like a dove and settling on him. And there came a voice from heaven. 'This is my Son, the Beloved and Only One,' the voice said, 'and on him my favour rests.'

Matthew 3:4–17

O Lord, make thy way plain before me. Let thy glory be my end. Thy Word my rule, and then, thy will be done.

KING CHARLES I

O God, give me the gift of perseverance.

If I fail in something the first time, help me to try and try
again, until I succeed.

If I have to do something difficult, help me not to get
discouraged, but to keep on trying.

If I find that results are slow to come, give me patience
that I may learn to wait.

Help me to remember that the more difficult a thing is,
the greater is the satisfaction in achieving it.

Help me to welcome every difficulty as a challenge and
an opportunity for victory; through Jesus Christ my
Lord. Amen.

### JESUS IN HIS HOME TOWN

He went to Nazareth, where he had been brought up, and,
as his habit was, he went into the synagogue on the Sabbath.
He rose to read the scripture lesson. The roll containing the
prophecies of Isaiah was handed to him. He unrolled the
roll and found the passage where it is written:

'The Spirit of the Lord is upon me,
because he has anointed me,
to bring good news to the poor.
He has sent me to announce to the prisoners
that they will be liberated,
and to the blind that they will see again,
to send away in freedom
those who have been broken by life,
to announce that the year
when the favour of God will be shown has come.'

He rolled up the roll, and handed it back to the officer.
He took the preacher's seat, and the eyes of everyone in the
synagogue were fixed intently on him. 'Today,' he said to
them, 'this passage of scripture has come true, as you
listened to it.'

They all agreed that the reports that they had heard of him were true, and they were astonished at the gracious words he spoke. 'Isn't this Joseph's son?' they said. He said: 'You are bound to quote the proverb to me, "Doctor, cure yourself." Do here in your home country all that we have heard about you doing in Capernaum.' He went on: 'This is the truth I tell you, no prophet is accepted in his own native place. You know quite well that it is the fact that there was many a widow in Israel in Elijah's time, when the sky was closed for three and a half years, and there was a severe famine all over the country; but to none of them was Elijah sent; he was sent to a widow in Sarepta in Sidon. There was many a leper in Israel in the time of Elisha; and none of them was cured; but Naaman the Syrian was.' The people in the synagogue were all enraged, when they heard him speak like this. They rose from their seats and hustled him out of the town. They took him to the brow of the hill on which their town is built, to hurl him down. But he walked straight through the middle of them, and went on his way.

Luke 4:16–30

O Lord God, when thou givest to thy servants to endeavour any great matter, grant us to know that it is not the beginning but the continuing of the same, until it be thoroughly finished, which yieldeth the true glory.

SIR FRANCIS DRAKE

Today, O God, I am free from my classes and my work.
Help me not to spend today in idleness, but to use it well.

Help me to engage in some game or activity which will
make me fitter in body.

Help me to use today to listen to some good music, to
read some good book, to see some good film or play, to
broaden my mind.

Help me to use today to spend some time with my friends.

Help me to use part of today to do something for someone else.

Help me to use today for such rest and relaxation as will
enable me to work and study better in the week to
come; through Jesus Christ my Lord. Amen.

### JESUS AND A CENTURION

When Jesus came into Capernaum, a centurion came up to
him with an urgent appeal. 'Sir,' he said, 'my servant is
lying at home paralysed and in terrible pain.' 'I will come
and cure him,' Jesus said. 'Sir,' answered the centurion, 'I
am not fit to have you come into my house. All I ask you to
do is to say the word, and my servant will be cured. For I
too know what it is to be under authority, and I have
soldiers under my command. I am used to saying to one,
"Go" and he goes, and to another, "Come here" and he
comes, and to my slave, "Do this" and he does it.' Jesus was
astonished to hear this. 'I tell you truly,' he said to those
who were following him, 'I have not found anyone in Israel
with a faith like this. I tell you that many will come from
the east and the west and will be fellow-guests with Abraham and Isaac and Jacob in the Kingdom of Heaven, but

those who were born to be members of the Kingdom will be flung out into the outer darkness, where there will be tears and agony. Go,' Jesus said to the centurion. 'Because you have a faith like this, your prayer is granted.' And the servant was cured at that very hour.

Matthew 8:5–13

O Lord Jesus Christ, who hast given thy life to redeem me, thyself for my example, thy word for my rule, thy grace for my guide, thy body on the cross for the sin of my soul: enter in and take possession of my heart, and dwell with me for ever. **After JEREMY TAYLOR**

O God, Sunday is the day which ought to be different from other days. Help me to make it so.

Help me to use today to think more definitely about you. Help me to worship with your people today. And if I don't worship in church, help me to find a few minutes to be alone, and to see you in the beauty of the world you have made.

On this, your day, help me to remember you. This I ask for your love's sake. Amen.

## THE KIND OF PEOPLE JESUS WANTS

As Jesus was walking along from there, he saw a man called Matthew, sitting in the office where he collected the customs duties. 'Follow me!' he said. And Matthew rose from his seat and followed him.

Jesus was sitting at a meal in the house, and many tax-collectors and people with whom no respectable Jew would have had anything to do came to be guests along with Jesus and his disciples. When the Pharisees saw this, they said to the disciples: 'Why does your Teacher eat with tax-collectors and with people with whom no respectable Jew would have anything to do?' Jesus heard this. 'It is not those who are well who need a doctor,' he said, 'but those who are ill. Go and learn the meaning of the saying, "It is mercy I want, not sacrifice." For I did not come to bring an invitation to those who are good but to those who are sinners.'

Matthew 9:9–13

Give unto us, O Lord, we humbly beseech thee, a wise, a sober, a patient, an understanding, a devout, a religious, a courageous heart; a soul full of devotion to do thee service, strength against all temptations; through Jesus Christ our Lord. Amen. ARCHBISHOP LAUD

Thank you, O God, for another day.
   Help me to spend it wisely and to spend it well.
Grant that everything I do today
   may be done as well as I can do it.
Grant that everyone I meet
   may be happier for the meeting.
Keep me all through today
   conscientious in my work;
   truthful in my speaking;
   loyal to my friends;
   faithful to those who love me;
   through Jesus Christ my Lord. Amen.

### MARCHING ORDERS

'You must not suppose that the result of my coming will be peace for the world. The result of my coming will not be peace but a sword. My coming is bound to result in a cleavage between a man and his father, between a daughter and her mother, between a daughter-in-law and her mother-in-law. A man's enemies will be his own kith and kin.

'If a man loves his father and mother more than he loves me, he is not fit to belong to me. If a man loves his son or daughter more than he loves me, he is not fit to belong to me. If a man does not take up his cross and follow in my footsteps, he is not fit to belong to me. To find your life is to lose it, and to lose it for my sake is to find it.'

Matthew 10:34–39

O Lord Jesus Christ, who art the way, the truth, and the life, we pray thee suffer us not to stray from thee, who art the way, nor to distrust thee, who art the truth, nor to rest in any other thing than thee, who are the life. Teach us by thy Holy Spirit what to believe, what to do, and wherein to take our rest. For thine own name's sake we ask it. Amen.

ERASMUS

O God, make me good at learning.

Give me the concentration of mind and the retentive memory I need to learn my lessons and my trade.

Help me to learn from advice, and to pay attention to people who have walked the road before and who know its pitfalls.

Help me to learn from experience and grant that I may not make the same mistakes over again until they become habits.

Help me each day to make myself a little better and a little wiser; through Jesus Christ my Lord. Amen.

THE ULTIMATE PROOF

When news of the things that the Messiah was doing reached John in prison, he sent his disciples to ask him: 'Are you the One who is to come, or are we to go on waiting and hoping for someone else?' 'Go,' answered Jesus, 'and tell John the story of all you are hearing and seeing. Blind men are seeing again; lame men are walking; lepers are being cleansed; deaf men are hearing; dead men are being raised to life; poor men are hearing the Good News. And happy is the man who does not find himself antagonized by me.'

Matthew 11:2–6

May God the Father bless us; may Christ take care of us; the Holy Ghost enlighten us all the days of our life. The Lord be our defender and keeper of body and soul, both now and for ever, to the ages of ages. Amen.

AEDELWALD

O God, you have given me life. Help me to give to people
what I ought to give:
    To my teachers, respect and attention;
    to my employers, diligence and honest service;
    to my parents, love and obedience;
    to my friends, loyalty and reliability;
    to everyone, friendliness and helpfulness.

Help me to give to each part of my life what I ought to give:
    To learning, concentration;
    to work, always my best effort;
    to my home, considerateness;
    to pleasure, purity;
    to love, fidelity.

Help me to live life as it ought to be lived, so that at the end
    I may have no regrets; through Jesus Christ my Lord.
    Amen.

THE RESPONSIBILITY OF PRIVILEGE
It was then that Jesus reproached the towns in which very
many of his miracles had been performed, because they
refused to repent. 'Tragic will be your fate, Chorazin!
Tragic will be your fate, Bethsaida! For, if the miracles
which have been done in you had been done in Tyre and
Sidon, they would long ago have repented in sackcloth and
ashes. But I tell you, Tyre and Sidon will get off more
lightly in the day of judgement than you. And you,
Capernaum – do you think you are going to be exalted as
high as heaven? You will go down to the depths of hell. For,
if the miracles which have been done in you had been done
in Sodom, it would still be standing today. But I tell you,

the land of Sodom will get off more lightly in the day of judgement than you!'

Matthew 11:20–24

Almighty and merciful God, the fountain of all goodness, who knowest the thoughts of our hearts, we confess unto thee that we have sinned against thee, and done evil in thy sight. Wash us, we beseech thee, from the stains of our past sins, and give us grace and power to put away all hurtful things, so that, being delivered from the bondage of sin, we may bring forth worthy fruits of repentance. O Eternal Light, shine into our hearts. O Eternal Goodness, deliver us from evil. O Eternal Power, be thou our support. Eternal Wisdom, scatter the darkness of our ignorance. Eternal Pity, have mercy upon us. Grant unto us, that with all our hearts, and minds, and strength, we may evermore seek thy face; and finally, bring us, in thine infinite mercy, to thy holy presence. So strengthen our weakness, that, following in the footsteps of thy blessed Son, we may obtain thy mercy, and enter into thy promised joy; through the same Jesus Christ, our only saviour and redeemer. Amen.

A. F. ALCUINUS

O God, help me to conquer the things which would keep me from being what I can be, and what I ought to be:

The inattention which makes me let things go in at one ear and out at the other;

The careless workmanship which does not put its best into every job;

The self-will which makes me resent and refuse guidance, and makes me take my own way – so often to trouble;

The laziness which makes me do nothing when all kinds of things are needing to be done;

The ingratitude which hurts those who have been kind to me;

The cowardice which makes me go with the crowd because I am afraid to stand alone;

The disloyalty which makes me let down my friends and disappoint those who love me –

Preserve me from all these things, O God. Strengthen me where I am weak; correct me where I am wrong; cleanse and purify me from all the faults which spoil my life; through Jesus Christ my Lord. Amen.

### THE GROWTH OF OPPOSITION

'If you had known the meaning of the saying, "It is mercy I want, not sacrifice," you would not have condemned those who are blameless, for the Son of Man's authority extends over the Sabbath.'

He moved on from there, and went into their synagogue. There was a man there with a withered hand. In an attempt to find something which they could use as a charge against him, they asked him: 'Is it permitted to heal on the Sabbath day?' 'If one of you has a sheep,' he said, 'and the sheep falls into a hole in the ground on the Sabbath day, will he not take a grip of it and lift it out? Surely you will admit that a man is more valuable than a sheep? Obviously, there is no law to stop a man doing good on the Sabbath day.' Then he said to the man: 'Stretch out your hand!' He stretched it out, and it was restored, healthy as the other. The Pharisees went away and concocted a scheme to kill him.

Matthew 12:7-14

Lord Jesus, by the indwelling of thy most Holy Spirit, purge our eyes to discern and contemplate thee until we attain to see as thou seest, judge as thou judgest, choose as thou choosest, and having sought and found thee, to behold thee for ever and ever. We ask this for thy name's sake. Amen.

CHRISTINA G. ROSSETTI

Forgive me, O God, for all the things for which I am sorry now:

For things I said, which were not true, which were not pure, which were not kind;
For things I did which were not honourable, which were not honest, which were not straight;
For people I hurt by being thoughtless and insensitive, by being selfish and inconsiderate, by being cruel and callous and deliberately wounding;

Forgive me, O God.

Help me from now on to keep a watch on my deeds and words so that I may never bring grief to others or sorrow to myself; through Jesus Christ my Lord. Amen.


THE SEED AND THE SOIL

On that day Jesus went out of the house and sat by the lake-side. Such crowds gathered to listen to him that he got into a boat and sat in it, while the crowd all stood on the shore. He used parables to tell them many things.

'Look!' he said. 'A sower went out to sow his seed. As he sowed, some seeds fell by the side of the road, and the birds came and snapped them up. Others fell on ground where there was only a thin skin of earth over the rock, and, because the soil was so shallow, they sprang up immediately, but when the sun rose, they were scorched, and they withered, because they had no root. Some fell among thorn-bushes, and the thorn-bushes shot up and choked the life out of them. Others fell on good ground, and produced a crop, some a hundred times, some sixty times, some thirty times as much as had been sown. If a man has ears, let him hear.'

Matthew 13:1–9

Almighty God, the giver of all good things, without whose help all labour is ineffectual, and without whose grace all wisdom is folly, grant, we beseech thee, that in all our undertakings, thy Holy Spirit may not be withheld from us: but that we may promote thy glory, and the salvation both of ourselves and others. Grant this, O Lord, for the sake of Jesus Christ our Lord. Amen.

SAMUEL JOHNSON

Lord Jesus, help me to have the same attitude to others as you had.

Give me a quick eye to see when others need help, and a ready hand to offer help where it is needed.

Give me a heart which is not cold but warm, a heart that is easily touched and moved at the sight of someone in sorrow or in need.

Give me the gift of sympathy so that I may never regard an appeal for help as a nuisance but rather as an opportunity.

Give me a feeling of responsibility to be a good example to those who are younger than I am. Give me respect to those who are older. And give me courtesy to everyone.

This I ask for your love's sake. Amen.

**FROM SMALL BEGINNINGS**

Jesus gave them another parable to think about. 'The Kingdom of Heaven,' he said, 'is like a grain of mustard seed, which a man took and sowed in his field. It is the smallest of all seeds, but when it has reached full growth, it becomes the biggest of all kitchen herbs, and grows into a tree big enough for the birds of the sky to come and nest among its branches.'

He told them another parable. 'The Kingdom of Heaven works like a piece of leaven,' he said, 'which a woman took and inserted into three pecks of flour, with the result that it was all leavened.'

Matthew 13:31–33

O Lord, lift up the light of thy countenance upon us; let thy peace rule in our hearts, and may it be our strength and our song, in the house of our pilgrimage. We commit ourselves to thy care and keeping this day; let thy grace be mighty in us, and sufficient for us, and let it work in us both to will and to do of thine own good pleasure, and grant us strength for all the duties of the day. Keep us from sin. Give us the rule over our own spirits, and keep us from speaking unadvisedly with our lips. May we live together in peace and holy love, and do thou command thy blessing upon us, even life for ever more. Prepare us for all the events of the day, for we know not what a day may bring forth. Give us grace to deny ourselves; to take up our cross daily, and to follow in the steps of our Lord and master, Jesus Christ our Lord. Amen.

MATTHEW HENRY

O God, I thank you that you have made me as I am.

> I thank you for a healthy body. Help me never to develop habits or to indulge in pleasures which would make me physically less fit.
> I thank you for a healthy mind. Help me to use it to keep learning things, and to think until I reach an answer to my problems.
> I thank you for all the interest of life, that there are always new things to do and to see.
> I thank you for the people who mean much to me – my friends, my teachers, my father and mother. Help me to live so that I will never disappoint them; through Jesus Christ my Lord. Amen.

GOD'S PLENTY

When he disembarked, he saw a great crowd, and he was heart-sorry for them, and cured their sick. Late on in the day the disciples came to him. 'This place is a desert,' they said, 'and it is now past the time for the evening meal. Send the crowd away into the villages to buy themselves food.' 'There is no necessity for them to go away,' Jesus said. 'You must give them something to eat.' 'All that we have here,' they said to him, 'is five loaves and two fishes.' 'Bring them to me,' Jesus said. So he ordered the crowd to sit down on the grass. He took the five loaves and the two fishes. He looked up to heaven and said the blessing. He broke the loaves into pieces and gave them to the disciples, and the disciples gave them to the crowds. They all ate until they could eat no more. They collected twelve basketfuls of pieces of bread that were left over. Those who ate numbered about five thousand men, not counting women and children.

Matthew 14:14-21

We beseech thee, O Lord, in thy loving-kindness, to pour thy holy light into our souls; that we may ever be devoted to thee, by whose wisdom we were created, and by whose providence we are governed; through Jesus Christ our Lord. Amen.

GELASIAN SACRAMENTARY

O God, bless all the people for whom life is hard and
difficult.
Those who are ill and who must lie in bed at home or in
hospital;
Those who cannot walk or run or jump and play games;
Those who are lonely because they are away from home;
Those who are sad because someone they loved has died;
Those who are not very clever and for whom it is a struggle
to keep up with the rest of the class;
Those who are shy and who find it difficult to meet people;
Those who are poor and who never have enough.

Help me, O God, to remember all such people, and to do
all I can to help them; through Jesus Christ my Lord.
Amen.

### JESUS AND A CANAANITE

Jesus left there and withdrew to the districts of Tyre and
Sidon. A Canaanite woman from these parts came to him.
'Take pity on me, sir, Son of David,' she kept shouting. 'My
daughter is possessed by a demon and is very ill.' Jesus did
not answer her at all. His disciples came and asked him:
'Send her away. She won't stop following us and shouting at
us.' Jesus said: 'It is only to the lost sheep of the family of
Israel that I have been sent.' She came and knelt in front of
him in entreaty. 'Sir,' she said, 'help me.' 'It is not proper,'
Jesus answered, 'to take the bread which belongs to the
children and to fling it to the pet dogs.' 'True, sir,' she
said, 'but the pet dogs do eat their share of the crumbs

which fall from their master's table.' At that Jesus answered: 'You have great faith. Let your wish be granted.' From that moment her daughter was cured.

Matthew 15:21–28

From the unreal lead me to the real;
from darkness lead me to light;
from death lead me to deathlessness.

Ancient Indian Prayer

O God, keep me from the things which would spoil life for myself and for others.

Keep me from procrastination, from putting things off until tomorrow. Whatever I have to do, help me to do it now, in case it is too late to do it at all.

Save me from the quick temper which would make me do and say things for which I would afterwards be very sorry.

Save me from the disobliging spirit, and when I am asked to do anything, help me to do it at once and to do it with a good grace.

Save me from being envious and discontented.

Help me to do the best I can with the things I have and with myself as I am.

Save me from being moody and irritable, and help me to meet life with a smile; through Jesus Christ my Lord. Amen.

### THE GREAT RECOGNITION

When Jesus had come to the districts of Caesarea Philippi, he put a question to his disciples. 'Who are people saying that the Son of Man is?' he asked. They said: 'Some are saying, John the Baptizer; others, Elijah; others, Jeremiah, or one of the prophets.' 'And you,' he said to them, 'who do you say that I am?' Simon Peter answered: 'You are the Messiah, the Son of the living God!' 'You are indeed blessed, Simon Barjona,' Jesus said, 'for it was no human being who revealed this to you; it was my Father who is in heaven. I tell you, you are Peter – the man whose name means a rock – and on this rock I will erect my Church, and the powers of death will be helpless to harm it. I will give you the keys of the Kingdom of Heaven, and whatever you forbid on earth will be forbidden in heaven, and

whatever you allow on earth will be allowed in heaven.'
Jesus gave strict orders to his disciples not to tell anyone
that he was the Messiah.

Matthew 16:13-20

O God, who by thy Spirit in our hearts dost lead men to
desire thy perfection, to seek for truths and to rejoice in
beauty: illuminate and inspire, we beseech thee, all thinkers,
writers, artists and craftsmen; that, in whatsoever is true
and pure and lovely, thy name may be hallowed and thy
kingdom come on earth; through Jesus Christ our Lord.

Prayer found in St Anselm's Chapel, Canterbury

O God, bless our country.

Bless those who are in Parliament, in the Cabinet; those who serve as permanent officials in the departments of state.

Grant that they may have no unworthy ambitions in which they are out for their own glory and their own profit; but grant that their ambition may be to make this a Christian country, in which men shall walk in the freedom of truth and the light of knowledge, a country in which none shall have too little and none too much.

Help me to be a good citizen of my country, doing an honest day's work, willing some day to take my part in the government of my city, my town, my district, my region.

Save me from being one of the many people who take everything and who give nothing.

Make me grateful for all that I have received, and determined to hand it on still better; through Jesus Christ my Lord. Amen.

ON LOSING AND SAVING ONE'S SOUL

Jesus went on to say to his disciples: 'If anyone wishes to walk in my steps, he must once and for all say No to himself; he must decide to take up his cross, and he must keep on following me. Anyone who wishes to keep his life safe will lose it, but anyone who is prepared to lose his life for my sake will find it. What good will it do to a man to gain the whole world, if in so doing he forfeits his own life? What could a man give that would be an equal exchange for his life? For the Son of Man will come with his angels in his

Father's glory, and he will settle accounts with each man on the basis of how each man has lived. I tell you truly, there are some of those who are standing here who will not experience death until they see the Son of Man coming in his Kingdom.'

Matthew 16:24–28


We commend unto thee, O Lord,
    our souls and our bodies,
    our minds and our thoughts,
    our prayers and our hopes,
    our health and our work,
    our life and our death,
    our parents and brothers and sisters,
    our benefactors and friends,
    our neighbours, our countrymen,
      and all Christian folk
        this day and always.

LANCELOT ANDREWES

Help me, O God, to try to make the work of other people easier and not harder.

At home, help me to be careful and tidy, cheerful and willing to take my share of the household chores.

At school, help me to behave well, and to work and study conscientiously.

At games, grant that I may never be guilty of any unfair action; grant that I would rather lose than win by a foul.

Where there are rules and regulations, help me to keep them and not to cause trouble by breaking them; through Jesus Christ my Lord. Amen.

#### THE TRANSFIGURATION

About a week later Jesus took with him Peter and James and John, James's brother, and brought them up into a high mountain alone. He was transformed before their very eyes. His face shone like the sun, and his clothes became as white as the light. Moses and Elijah appeared to them, talking to Jesus. 'Master,' Peter said to Jesus, 'it is a wonderful thing for us to be here. Would you like me to make three shelters here, one for you, one for Moses, and one for Elijah?' While he was still speaking, a shining cloud enveloped them, and out of the cloud a voice said: 'This is my Son, the Beloved and Only One, on whom my favour rests. Listen to him!' When the disciples heard this, they flung themselves face down on the ground, for they were terrified. Jesus came and touched them. 'Up!' he said. 'Don't be afraid!' And when they looked up, the only person they could see was Jesus, all by himself.

Matthew 17:1–8

O thou almighty will
Faint are thy children, till
   Thou come with power:
Strength of our good intents,
In our frail home, defence,
Calm of faith's confidence,
   Come, in this hour!

O thou most tender love!
Deep in our spirits move:
   Tarry, dear guest!
Quench thou our passion's fire,
Raise thou each low desire,
Deeds of brave love inspire,
   Quickener and rest!

O light serene and still!
Come, and our spirit fill,
   Bring in the day:
Guide of our feeble sight,
Star of our darkest night,
Shine on the path of right,
   Show us the way!

                    KING ROBERT OF FRANCE

Help me, O God, to banish self from life:

The selfishness which makes me the centre of the whole universe;
The self-conceit which thinks far too highly of itself;
The self-will which resents and refuses all advice;
The self-pity which is sorry for itself;
The self-deception which refuses to see itself as it is;
The self-abasement which is only an excuse to shirk my duties and my responsibilities;
The self-excusing which always puts the blame on someone else;

Help me to be done with all these; through Jesus Christ my Lord. Amen.

### JESUS AND THE EPILEPTIC BOY

When they reached the crowd, a man came to Jesus and knelt at his feet. 'Sir,' he said, 'take pity on my son. He is an epileptic, and he is very ill. He often falls into the fire and into the water. And I brought him to your disciples, and they were quite unable to cure him.' 'This modern generation has no faith,' Jesus answered. 'There is a fatal perversity about it. How long have I to be with you? How long must I endure you? Bring him here to me!' Then Jesus spoke to him with a stern authority, and the demon came out of him, and there and then the boy was cured. Afterwards when they were alone, the disciples came to Jesus. 'Why were we unable to eject the demon?' they asked him. 'Because,' he said, 'you have so little faith. I tell you truly, if you have faith as big as a mustard seed, you will say to this mountain: "Move from here to there," and it will remove itself. There will be nothing you cannot do.'

Matthew 17:14–21

Lord, give us to go blithely on our business all this day, bring us to our resting beds weary and content and undishonoured, and grant us in the end the gift of sleep.

ROBERT LOUIS STEVENSON

O God, who has folded back the mantle of the night, to clothe us in the golden glory of the day, chase from our hearts all gloomy thoughts, and make us glad with the brightness of hope, that we may effectively aspire to unwon virtues; through Jesus Christ our Lord.

Ancient Collect

O God, this is Saturday, the day when I don't need to go out to school or to work. It is the day when I can do what I like. Help me to make good use of it.

Help me to use it for rest, without being lazy.

If I use it to play games, help me to play hard but to play clean.

If I use it to spectate, help me to enjoy it, and to support my team without being a fanatic about it.

If I go to the cinema or to the theatre, or if I listen to music or go dancing, help me to enjoy it to the full and to remain well-behaved.

Help me to use this Saturday to be refreshed in body and stimulated in mind; through Jesus Christ my Lord. Amen.

FORGIVE TO BE FORGIVEN

Peter came to Jesus. 'Master,' he said to him, 'how often ought I to forgive my fellow man, if he goes on wronging me? As many as seven times?' 'I tell you,' Jesus said to him, 'not as many as seven times, but as many as seventy times seven. That is why what happens in the Kingdom of Heaven can be compared with the situation which arose when a king wished to settle accounts with his servants. When he began to settle up, one debtor was brought in who owed him two and a half million pounds. He was quite unable to pay. So his master gave orders for him to be sold, along with his wife and children and everything he had, and the money to be paid over. The servant threw himself on his knees at his master's feet. "Give me time," he said, "and I will pay you everything in full." The servant's master was heart-sorry for the man, and let him go free, and remitted the debt. That same servant went out and met one of his fellow-servants who owed him five pounds. He seized him by the throat. "Pay your debt'!' he said. His fellow-servant threw himself at his feet. "Give me time," he begged, "and I will pay you in full." He refused, and went and had him thrown into prison, until he should pay the debt in full. When his fellow-servants saw what had happened, they were very distressed. So they went to their master and informed him of all that had happened. The master sent for the servant. "You utter scoundrel!" he said. "I remitted that whole debt of yours, because you pleaded with me to do so. Surely you should have had the same pity for your fellow-servant as I had for you." The master was furious, and handed him over to the torturers until he should repay the whole debt in full. My heavenly Father will do the same to you, if you do not, each one of you, genuinely forgive your fellow man.'

Matthew 18:21–35

O Lord God Almighty, I charge thee of thy great mercy and by the token of thy holy rood that thou guide me to thy will and to my soul's need better than I can myself, that above all things I may inwardly love thee with a clear mind and clean body; for thou art my maker, my help and my hope.

KING ALFRED THE GREAT

O God, help me to remember that this is the Lord's Day, and help me to remember that it is called that because it is the day on which Jesus rose from the dead.

So help me to remember that Jesus is not just a person in a book, but that he is here always although we cannot see him. He is here to warn us in any time of temptation and to help us in any time of difficulty.

Help us to remember that he is the unseen companion of all my way, and the unseen guest in every home. This I ask for your love's sake. Amen.

### THE ONE THING LACKING

A man came to Jesus. 'Teacher,' he said, 'what must I do to make myself good enough to possess eternal life?' 'Why do you ask me about what is good?' Jesus said to him. 'One and One alone is good. If you want to get into life, obey the commandments.' 'What commandments?' he said. Jesus said: 'The commandments which say: You must not kill, You must not commit adultery, You must not steal, You must not tell lies about anyone, Honour your father and your mother, and, You must love your neighbour as yourself.' 'I have obeyed all these,' the young man said to him. 'What is still missing in me?' 'If you really want to be perfect,' Jesus said to him, 'go and sell everything you have and give the proceeds to the poor, and you will have treasure in heaven. Then come! Follow me!' When the young man heard Jesus say this, he went sadly away, for he was very wealthy.

Matthew 19:16–22

Merciful God, be thou now unto us a strong tower of defence. Give us grace to await thy leisure, and patiently to bear what thou doest unto us, nothing doubting thy goodness towards us. Therefore do with us in all things as thou wilt: Only arm us, we beseech thee, with thy armour, that we may stand fast; above all things taking to us the shield of faith, praying always that we may refer ourselves wholly to thy will, being assuredly persuaded that all thou doest cannot but be well. And unto thee be all honour and glory.

LADY JANE GREY

O God, it is back to work and back to study today.

Whatever I have to do, help me to put my best into it. Even when work is dull, help me to do it well, always remembering that to do today's work well is to be on the way to more interesting work tomorrow.

Help me to remember that there is no easy way to the top, and that I will only get there by doing each day's work as well as it can be done, whatever it may be; through Jesus Christ my Lord. Amen.

MASTER OR SERVANT? WHICH IS YOUR AMBITION?
It was then the mother of Zebedee's sons came to him with her sons. She knelt before him and asked him to give her a special favour. 'What is it you want?' he said to her. 'I want my two sons,' she said, 'to sit one on your right hand and one on your left in your Kingdom.' 'You do not know what you are asking for,' Jesus said. 'Can you pass through the bitter experience through which I must pass?' 'We can,' they said. He said to them: 'You will pass through the same experience as I must go through, but to sit on my right hand and on my left is not in my power to give you. That is reserved for those for whom it has been prepared by my Father.'

When the ten heard about this, they were annoyed with the two brothers. Jesus called them to him. 'You know,' he said, 'that the leaders of the Gentiles lord it over them, and that in their society the mark of greatness is the exercise of authority. But in your society the situation is very different. With you, if anyone wishes to be great, he must be your servant; and with you, if anyone wishes to hold the first place, he must be everyone's slave, just as the Son of Man did not come to be served but to serve, and to give his life as a ransom for many.'

Matthew 20:20–28

O Lord, make thy way plain before me. Let thy glory be my end. Thy word my rule, and then, thy will be done.

KING CHARLES I

O God, keep me from being difficult to live with.

Keep me from being irritable, and from losing my temper about trifles.

Keep me from being moody and unpredictable.

Keep me from being far too critical of others, and of what they do for me.

Keep me from being so self-centred that I cannot see that anyone else can ever be right.

Keep me from being rude and impolite, and help me at all times to be courteous in manner and in speech.

Help me always to do and be to others what I would wish them to do and be to me; through Jesus Christ my Lord. Amen.

### SIGHT FOR FAITH

They were leaving Jericho followed by a large crowd. There were two blind men sitting at the roadside. When they heard that Jesus was passing, they shouted: 'Master! Take pity on us! Son of David!' The crowd sharply told them to be quiet, but they shouted all the louder: 'Master! Take pity on us! Son of David!' Jesus stopped and called them. 'What do you want me to do for you?' he said. 'Sir,' they said to him, 'the only thing we want is to be able to see.' Jesus was heart-sorry for them. He touched their eyes, and there and then their sight returned, and they followed him.

Matthew 20:29–34

Keep me, O Lord, while I tarry on this earth, in a daily serious seeking after thee, and in a believing affectionate walking with thee; that, when thou comest, I may be found not hiding my talent, nor serving my flesh, nor yet asleep with my lamp unfurnished; but waiting and longing for my Lord, my glorious God, for ever and ever.

RICHARD BAXTER

O God, help me to find my pleasure in the right things and in the right way.

Grant that I may never look for pleasure in anything that would make my body less fit, my mind less efficient, or my heart less pure.

Grant that I may never look for pleasure in anything which would damage things or injure people.

Grant that I may never look for pleasure in things which would lead others astray or make it easier for them to go wrong.

Grant that I may never look for pleasure in things which would afterwards bring regret or make me sorry.

Help me always to find pleasure in things which hurt no one and which bring no regrets to follow; through Jesus Christ my Lord. Amen.

### THE TRIUMPHAL ENTRY

When they were near Jerusalem, and when they had reached Bethphage, at the Hill of Olives, Jesus sent on two of his disciples. 'Go into the village opposite you,' he said, 'and you will at once find a tethered donkey, and a foal with her. Untie them and bring them to me. If anyone says anything to you, you will say: "The Master needs them," and he will send them at once.' This happened so that the statement made through the prophet might come true:

'Say to the daughter of Sion:
"Look! Your king is coming to you,
gentle, and riding on an ass,
and on a colt, the foal of a beast of burden." '

The disciples went off and carried out Jesus' instructions. They brought the donkey and the foal. They put their cloaks on them and Jesus mounted them. The huge crowd spread their cloaks on the road, while others cut down branches from the trees, and spread them on the road. The crowds who were going on ahead and the crowds who were following behind kept shouting:

'God save David's Son!
God bless him who comes in the name of the Lord!
O send your salvation from the heights of heaven!'

When Jesus entered Jerusalem, the whole city seethed with excitement. 'Who is this?' they said. The crowds said: 'This is the prophet Jesus from Nazareth in Galilee.'

Matthew 21:1–11

Accept, O Lord God, our Father, the sacrifices of our thanksgiving; this, of praise, for thy great mercies already afforded to us; and this, of prayer, for the continuance and enlargement of them; this, of penitence, for such only recompense as our sinful nature can endeavour; and this, of the love of our hearts, as the only gift thou dost ask or desire; and all these, through the all-holy and atoning sacrifice of Jesus Christ thy Son, our saviour.

JOHN DONNE

Lord Jesus, give me the things I need to live life well:

Encouragement, when I feel that nothing is happening and that I am not getting anywhere;

Resistance power, when I feel the fascination of the wrong things;

The ability to stand up for what I believe is right, even if it means unpopularity and standing alone;

Perseverance, especially at the times when it would be easier to give up than to go on;

Honesty, that I may value truth above all things;

Self-respect, so that I may never lower myself to being less than my best;

Grant me these things, God; through Jesus Christ my Lord. Amen.

### THE CLEANSING OF THE TEMPLE

Jesus went into the Temple precincts, and drove out all who were selling and buying there, and upset the tables of the money-changers, and the seats of the pigeon-sellers. 'Scripture says,' he said to them, ' "My house must be regarded as a house of prayer," but you are making it a brigands' den.'

The blind and the lame came to him in the Temple precincts and he cured them. When the chief priests and the experts in the Law saw the astonishing things that Jesus did, and when they heard the children shouting in the Temple precincts: 'God save David's Son!' they were enraged. 'Do you hear what the children are saying?' they said to him. 'I do,' Jesus said to them. 'Have you never read:

"Out of the mouths of babes and sucklings you have brought perfect praise"?' So he left there, and went out of the city to Bethany, and spent the night there.

Matthew 21:12–17

Relieve and comfort, O Lord, all the persecuted and afflicted; speak peace to troubled consciences; strengthen the weak; confirm the strong; instruct the ignorant; deliver the oppressed from him that spoileth him; and relieve the needy that hath no helper; and bring us all, by the waters of comfort and in the ways of righteousness, to the kingdom of rest and glory; through Jesus Christ our Lord. Amen.

BISHOP JEREMY TAYLOR

O God, there is so much for which I ought to give thanks.

For life, and life in this beautiful and interesting world;
For parents and for a home and for all that is daily done
    for me;
For school and for teachers, for work to do, for all that
    equips me some day to earn a living for myself and for
    those who will be dependent on me;
For all happy and healthy pleasures which exercise my
    body and refresh my mind;
For the loyalty of friends, for the care of loved ones, and
    for your love to me in Jesus who lived and died for me:
    I thank you.
Accept my prayer through Jesus Christ my Lord. Amen.

### THE HEART

'Listen to another parable. There was a householder who
planted a vineyard. He surrounded it with a hedge, and dug
out a pit in which the juice could be extracted from the
grapes, and built a watch-tower. He then let it out to
tenants and went abroad. When the fruit season arrived, he
sent his servants to the tenants to receive his due share of the
crop. The tenants took the servants, and beat one up, and
killed another, and stoned another. Again he sent other
servants, more than the first lot he had sent, and they
treated them in the same way. He then sent his son to them.
"They will treat my son with respect," he said. But, when
the tenants saw the son, they said to themselves: "This is the
heir. Come on! Let's kill him! And let us seize his estate!"
So they took him, and threw him out of the vineyard and
killed him. When the owner of the vineyard comes, what
will he do to these tenants?' They said, 'He will see to it
that these bad men come to a bad end, and he will let out
the vineyard to other tenants, who will pay him his full share

of the crops when it is due.' Jesus said to them: 'Have you never read in the scriptures:

> "The stone which the builders rejected,
> this has become the headstone of the corner.
> This is the action of God,
> and it is marvellous in our eyes"?

I tell you, that is why the Kingdom of God will be taken from you, and given to a nation whose conduct befits it.'

Matthew 21:33-43

Glory be to thee, O Heavenly Father, for our being and preservation, health and strength, understanding and memory, friends and benefactors, and for all our abilities of mind and body. Glory be to thee for our competent livelihood, for the advantages of our education, for all known and unobserved deliverances, and for the guard which thy holy angels keep over us. Glory be to thee, O Lord, O Blessed Saviour, for those ordinary gifts by which sincere Christians have in all ages been enabled to work for their salvation, for all the spiritual strength and support, comfort and illumination which we receive from thee, and for all thy preserving, restraining, and sanctifying grace.

BISHOP THOMAS KEN

Save me from being altogether selfish in my prayers, and help me to remember others who are in trouble.

The sick and those who must lie in bed throughout the sunlit hours, especially young folk laid aside too soon in the morning of their day;

Those who are sad and sorry because someone they loved has died;

Those who are disappointed because something they wanted very much has passed them by;

The discontented, those who live with a chip on their shoulder, who are their own worst enemies;

Those who have done something wrong and who are in disgrace, that they may redeem themselves;

Those who are underrated and undervalued, and who have never been appreciated as they ought to have been;

Those who have been passed over for some office they had expected to receive;

All those in pain, in sorrow, in misfortune, in disgrace:

Bless all such. For your love's sake I ask it. Amen.

THE GUEST AND THE GARMENT

Once again Jesus spoke to them in parables. 'The situation in the Kingdom of Heaven,' he said, 'is like the situation which arose when a king gave a wedding banquet for his son. He sent out his servants to tell the guests, who had already received their invitations to the banquet, to come, and they refused to come. He sent out a second lot of servants. "Tell those who have been invited," he said, "that I have completed the preparations for the dinner I am giving. My oxen and specially fattened calves have been killed. Everything is ready. Come to the wedding banquet."

They completely disregarded the invitation, and went off, one to his farm and another to his business. The others seized the servants, and wantonly ill-treated them, and killed them. The king was furious and sent his troops and wiped out those murderers, and burned their town. Then he said to the servants: "The wedding banquet is all ready, but those who received invitations to it did not deserve them. Go out to the open roads and invite everyone you meet to the banquet." So the servants went out to the roads and collected everyone they met, good and bad alike, and so the room where the wedding banquet was to be held was filled with guests.

'When the king came in to look at the guests, he saw a man there who was not dressed in wedding clothes. "Friend," he said to him, "why have you come like this, without wedding clothes?" The man had nothing to say. Then the king said to the attendants: "Tie him up, hand and foot, and fling him out into the outer darkness." There will be tears and agony there. For many are invited but few are chosen.'

Matthew 22:1–14

Write thy blessed name, O Lord, upon my heart, there to remain so indelibly engraved, that no prosperity, no adversity shall ever move me from thy love. Be thou to me a strong tower of defence, a comforter in tribulation, a deliverer in distress, a very present help in trouble, and a guide to heaven through the many temptations and dangers of this life.  THOMAS À KEMPIS

Lord Jesus, this is your day. Help me to use at least some part of it to think of you.

Help me to remember that there are other things in life than material things, and that all the material things in the world cannot make me happy if I am not right myself.

Help me to remember that this is not the only world, and help me to live well in this world that I am prepared for the world to come.

Help me to remember that the things which are seen are temporary and passing, but the unseen things are eternal and last for ever.

So grant that I may live as always in the shadow of eternity remembering that there is a day of judgement, and that there is another world, and that what I do here will determine what life in that other world will be; through Jesus Christ my Lord. Amen.

CAESAR'S AND GOD'S

The Pharisees went and concocted a scheme to lay a verbal trap for Jesus. They sent their disciples to him along with Herod's supporters. 'Teacher,' they said to him, 'we know that you speak the truth, and that you really do teach the life that God wishes us to live. We know that it makes no difference to you who or what anyone is, and that man-made prestige means nothing to you. Well, then, tell us, what is your opinion – is it right for us to pay the poll-tax to Caesar, or is it not?' Jesus was well aware of their malicious motives. 'You are not out for information,' he said to them, 'you are out to make trouble in your two-faced maliciousness. Show me the coin with which the poll-tax is paid.' They brought him a silver piece. 'Whose portrait and whose inscription is this?' he asked. 'Caesar's,' they said. 'Well, then,' he said to them, 'pay to Caesar what belongs to Caesar, and to God what belongs to God.' When they heard that answer, they were astonished, and went away and left him.

Matthew 22:15–22

In confidence of thy goodness and great mercy, O Lord, I draw near unto thee, as a sick person to the healer, as one hungry and thirsty to the fountain of life, a creature to the creator, a desolate soul to my own tender comforter. Behold, in thee is all whatsoever I can or ought to desire; thou art my salvation and my redemption, my help and my strength. Rejoice therefore this day the soul of thy servant; for unto thee, O Lord, have I lifted up my soul.

THOMAS À KEMPIS

O God, bless and help all those who have to face life with some handicap.

Those who are lame and crippled, who cannot run and jump and play the games which other people play;
Those who are blind and who cannot see the light of the sun or the faces of their friends;
Those who are deaf, who cannot hear the voices of their friends, who cannot listen to music or the singing of the birds;
Those whose minds are disturbed and for whom the kindly light of reason burns dim;
Those who find learning difficult, and for whom it is a constant struggle to keep up with the class.

Give courage and strength and help to all those who are handicapped, and grant that those who are strong may be ever ready and willing to help them; through Jesus Christ our Lord. Amen.

**THE FIRST AND GREAT COMMANDMENT**
When the Pharisees heard that Jesus had silenced the Sadducees, they came in a body. One of them, a legal expert, put a question to Jesus as a test. 'Teacher,' he said, 'which is the greatest commandment in the Law?' Jesus said to him: 'You must love the Lord your God with your whole heart and your whole soul and your whole mind. This is the first and greatest commandment. And there is a second one like it: You must love your neighbour as yourself. On these two commandments the whole message of the Law and of the Prophets depends.'

Matthew 22:34-40

O living Christ, make us conscious now of thy healing nearness. Touch our eyes that we may see thee; open our ears that we may hear thy voice; enter our hearts that we may know thy love. Overshadow our souls and bodies with thy presence, that we may partake of thy strength, thy love and thy healing life.

H. C. ROBBINS

Lord Jesus, I thank you for the life you lived:
That you were born into an ordinary home;
That you did an ordinary job, when you were the village
carpenter of Nazareth;
That you were tempted to sin as all men are tempted,
and that you never fell to temptation;
That you loved the open air, and the flowers and the
birds, and the waters of the lake, and all men.

Lord Jesus, I thank you for the death you died:
That you loved men to the bitter end;
That you endured the worst that men could do to you,
and still forgave them;
That your death was for me and my salvation.

Lord Jesus, we thank you for your resurrection:
We thank you that you rose from the dead and that you
are alive for ever more to be the continual companion
of our way.

Hear this our thanksgiving for your love's sake. Amen.

ALAS FOR YOU!
'Tragic will be the fate of you experts in the Law and you
Pharisees with your façade of ostentatious piety! You roam
sea and land to make one convert, and, when he has become a convert, you make him twice as much hell-begotten
as yourselves.

'Tragic will be your fate, for you are blind guides! You say: "If a man swears by the Temple, there is no necessity to keep the oath, but, if a man swears by the gold of the Temple, he is bound to keep it." You are senseless and blind! Which is greater – the gold, or the Temple which makes the gold sacred? You say: "If a man swears by the altar, there is no necessity to keep the oath, but, if a man swears by the gift that is on it, he is bound to keep it." You are blind! Which is greater – the gift, or the altar which makes the gift sacred? If a man swears by the altar, he swears by it and by all that is on it. If a man swears by the Temple, he swears by it, and by him whose home it is. If a man swears by heaven, he swears by the throne of God, and by him who sits on it.

'Tragic will be the fate of you experts in the Law and you Pharisees with your façade of ostentatious piety! For you meticulously pay the tenth part of your crop of mint and dill and cummin to the Temple, and you completely neglect the more important demands of the Law – justice, mercy and loyalty. You ought to have kept the second without neglecting the first. You are blind guides, you who carefully filter a midge out of your drink and then swallow a camel!

'Tragic will be the fate of you experts in the Law and you Pharisees with your façade of ostentatious piety! For you carefully clean the outside of the cup and the plate while you leave the inside full to overflowing with greed and un-bridled self-indulgence. You blind Pharisee! First clean the inside of the cup, and then outside and inside will both be clean.'                                    Matthew 23:13–26

We thank thee, O Lord, for all who have chosen poverty or solitude for thy sake, for men of prayer, for saints in common life who have borne suffering for noble ends, and for those who have endured pain with patience and purity of life, in the strength of him who for the joy that was set before him endured the cross, ever Jesus Christ our Lord.          ANON

Save us, O God, from the folly of putting things off until
tomorrow or to some more distant date.

Save us from dodging the tasks we don't want to do.

Save us from shirking the things which are difficult to do.

Save us from putting things off that we are just too lazy to
do.

Save us from putting things off because we think that we
have plenty of time, and help us always to remember that
tomorrow may never come for us.

Help us to remember that all we do possess is the present
moment and that tomorrow is the most dangerous word
in the language.

Help us to remember now our creator in the days of our
youth, and to do things now; through Jesus Christ our
Lord. Amen.

ALAS FOR YOU!

'Tragic will be the fate of you experts in the Law and you
Pharisees with your façade of ostentatious piety! For you
are like white-washed tombs, which look beautiful from the
outside, but which are full of dead men's bones and all kinds
of filth. So you too, as far as external appearances go, seem
to people to be carefully obeying the Law, but you are really
putting on an act, for inside you are full of disobedience to
the Law.

'Tragic will be the fate of you experts in the Law and you
Pharisees with your façade of ostentatious piety! You build
tombs for the prophets and erect lovely memorials to good
men, and you say: "If we had lived in the days of our
ancestors, we would not have been partners with them in
the murder of the prophets." By your very statement you
provide evidence that you yourselves are the descendants of
those who killed the prophets. Carry on! Equal your fathers
in their sins! You serpents! You brood of vipers! How can
you escape being condemned to hell?

'Let me tell you why I send you prophets and sages and experts in the Law. Some of them you will kill and crucify. Some of them you will flog in your synagogues, and hunt from town to town. The reason is that there may rest on you the responsibility for the murder of every good man from the murder of the good Abel to the murder of Zachariah, Barachiah's son, between the Temple and the altar. I tell you, retribution for all this will descend upon the people of today.

'O Jerusalem, Jerusalem! Killer of the prophets! Stoner of those who were sent to you by God! How often I have wanted to gather your children together as a bird gathers her nestlings under the shelter of her wings – and you refused! God no longer has his home among you, for, I tell you, you will not see me again until you say: "God bless him who comes as the representative of the Lord." '

Matthew 23:27–39

Give me, O Lord, a steadfast heart, which no unworthy affection may drag downwards; give me an unconquered heart, which no tribulation can wear out; give me an upright heart, which no unworthy purpose may tempt aside. Bestow upon me also, O Lord my God, understanding to know thee, wisdom to find thee, and a faithfulness that may finally embrace thee.

THOMAS AQUINAS

O God, help me to love my neighbour as I love myself.

Help me never to bear grudges, but to put them out of my mind and to forget.

Help me never to look for revenge, because looking for revenge leads only to more trouble.

Help me always to love others, never to seek anything but their good, never to try to injure anyone but always to help. Even if I don't like a person, help me still to seek nothing but his good.

Help me to take Jesus as my example and to go about like him, doing good.

This I ask for your love's sake. Amen.

### TOO LATE!

'What will happen in the Kingdom of Heaven is like what happened to ten bridesmaids, who took their lamps and went out to meet the bridegroom. Five of them were foolish and five were sensible. The foolish ones brought their lamps, but they did not bring any oil with them. The sensible ones took oil in jars along with their lamps. When the bridegroom was a long time in coming, they grew drowsy. They were all asleep, when in the middle of the night there was a shout: "Here comes the bridegroom! Out you go and meet him!" At this all the girls woke up and trimmed their lamps. The foolish ones said to the sensible ones: "Our lamps have gone out. Give us some of your oil." "We can't do that," the sensible ones answered, "because then there might not be enough oil for us and for you. You had better go to those who sell oil, and buy some for yourselves." While they were away buying it, the bridegroom arrived. The bridesmaids who were ready went in to the banquet with him, and the door was shut. Later on the other girls arrived. "Sir!" they said, "Sir! Open the door for us!" "I tell you truly," he said, "I don't know who you are!" So, then, be sleeplessly on the watch, because you do not know the day or the hour.'

Matthew 25:1–13

# THURSDAY: FIFTH WEEK

Lord make me an instrument of thy peace.
Where there is hatred, let me sow love;
Where there is injury, pardon;
Where there is doubt, faith;
Where there is despair, hope;
Where there is darkness, light;
Where there is sadness, joy.

O Divine Master, grant that
I may not so much seek
To be consoled, as to console;
Not so much seek to be understood as
To understand;
Not so much seek to be
Loved as to love:
For it is in giving that we receive;
It is in pardoning, that we are pardoned;
It is in dying, that we awaken to eternal life.

ST FRANCIS OF ASSISI

Help me, O God, to sow in my life all the fruit of the Spirit:

Love, that I may live at peace with all men;

Joy, that I may be as happy as the day is long;

Peace, that I may never be worried and anxious;

Patience, that I may learn to wait upon events and to bear with people;

Gentleness, that I may always be kind;

Goodness, that I may be an example to all;

Fidelity, that I may always keep my promise and my word;

Meekness, that I may have every passion under strict control;

Self-control, that I may be master of myself and so be fit to serve others.

Grant me these things, O God; through Jesus Christ my Lord. Amen.

### USE IT OR LOSE IT

'After a long time the master of these servants returned and settled accounts with them. The man who had been given the twelve hundred and fifty pounds came up with another twelve hundred and fifty pounds. "Master," he said, "You handed over twelve hundred and fifty pounds to me. I have made a profit of another twelve hundred and fifty pounds." "Well done!" his master said to him. "You have shown yourself a good and trustworthy servant. Because you have shown that I could depend on you to do a small job well, I will give you a big job to do. Come and share your master's joy." The man who had been given the five hundred pounds came up. "Sir," he said, "you handed over five hundred pounds to me. I have made a profit of another five hundred pounds." "Well done!" his master said to him. "You have shown yourself to be a good and trustworthy servant. Because you have shown that I could depend on you to do a small job well, I will give you a big job to do. Come and share your master's joy."

'The man who had been given the two hundred and fifty pounds came up. "Sir," he said, "I am well aware that you are a shrewd and ruthless business man. I know that you have a habit of letting someone else do the work and of then taking the profits. I know you often step in and appropriate the results of some enterprise which you did not initiate. So I went and hid your two hundred and fifty pounds in a hole in the ground, because I was afraid to take the risk of doing anything with it. Here you are! Your money is safe!" "You lazy good-for-nothing!" his master answered. "You knew very well that I have a habit of letting other people do the work and of then taking the profits. You knew very well that I often step in and appropriate the results of some enterprise which I did not initiate. That is all the more reason why you ought to have lodged my money with the bankers, and then, when I came home, I would have got my money back with interest. Take the two hundred and fifty pounds from him, and give it to the man who has two thousand five hundred pounds. For, if any man has much, he will be given still more, but, if any man has nothing, he will lose even what he has. Fling the useless servant out into outer darkness. There will be tears and agony there." '

Matthew 25:14–30

I bind unto myself today
The power of God to hold and lead,
His eye to watch, his might to stay,
His ear to hearken to my need.
The wisdom of my God to teach,
His hand to guide, his shield to ward,
The word of God to give me speech,
His heavenly host to be my guard.

St Patrick's Breastplate Stanza 1

O God, give me wisdom,
    that I may always be able to know what is right to do,
    that I may be able to distinguish between that which is
        momentarily pleasant and that which is of lasting good.
Give me courage,
    always to do the right thing even when I am afraid to do
    it.
Give me self-control,
    so that no moment of impulse or passion may sweep me
    into mistakes I would regret.
Above all, give me love,
    that I may love all men as you love them, and that there
    should be no hatred in my heart.
        Through Jesus Christ my Lord. Amen.

HELPING JESUS

'When the Son of Man comes in his glory, accompanied by all the angels, he will take his seat on his glorious throne. The people of every nation will be assembled before him, and he will separate them into two groups, in the same way as a shepherd separates the sheep from the goats. He will place the sheep on the right hand and the goats on the left. Then the king will say to those on the right: "You have earned my Father's blessing. Come and take possession of the kingdom, which has been prepared for you since the creation of the world. For, when I was hungry, you gave me food to eat; when I was thirsty, you gave me water to drink; when I was a stranger, you took me into your home circle; when I was naked, you clothed me; when I was ill, you came to visit me; when I was in prison, you came to see me." Then the good people will answer: "Sir, when did we see you hungry and feed you, or thirsty and give you water to drink? When did we see you a stranger and take you into our home circle, or naked and clothe you? When did we see you ill or in prison and come to visit you?" The king will answer: "The truth is that every time you did these things for one of my brothers, even for the least of them, you did them for me." Then he will say to those on the left: "God's curse is on you! Begone to the eternal fire which has been prepared for the devil and his angels! For, when I was hungry, you did not give me food to eat; when I was thirsty, you did not give me water to drink; when I was a stranger, you did not take me into your home circle; when I was naked, you did not clothe me; when I was ill and in prison, you did not come to visit me." At that, they will answer: "Sir, when did we see you hungry or thirsty or a stranger or naked or ill or in prison, and fail to give you help?" Then he will answer: "The truth is that every time you failed to do these things for one of these, even for the least of them, you failed to do them for me." These will go away to eternal punishment, but the good will go to eternal life.'

Matthew 25:31-46

Christ be with me, Christ within me,
Christ behind me, Christ before me,
Christ beside me, Christ to win me,
Christ to comfort and restore me.
Christ beneath me, Christ above me,
Christ in quiet, Christ in danger,
Christ in hearts of all that love me,
Christ in mouth of friend and stranger.

St Patrick's Breastplate Stanza 2

O God, help me to make this a day of rest, when I lay aside my studies and my work so that I may go back to them tomorrow refreshed.

Help me to make it a day of gladness, because I am glad that on this day Jesus rose from the dead.

Help me to make it a day of learning, when I try to find out something new about life and how to live it.

Help me to make it a day of friendship, when I spend some time in my home and with my friends.

Help me to make it a day of worship, when I think about you and remember your presence:

through Jesus Christ my Lord. Amen.

#### TREACHERY

It was then that the chief priests and the elders of the people met in the palace of the High Priest, whose name was Caiaphas, and discussed how to arrest Jesus by some stratagem, and so to kill him. Their problem was that they could not arrest him during the festival, because they could not take the risk of a popular riot breaking out among the people.

It was at this time that one of the Twelve, called Judas Iscariot, went to the chief priests. 'What are you prepared to give me,' he said, 'if I deliver him into your hands?' They settled with him for five pounds. From then on Judas was always looking for a good opportunity to deliver Jesus into their hands.

Matthew 26:3–5 and 14–16

Fill us, we pray thee, with thy light and life, that we may show forth thy wondrous glory. Grant that thy love may so fill our lives that we may count nothing too small to do for thee, nothing too much to give, and nothing too hard to bear. So teach us, Lord, to serve thee as thou deservest, to give and not to count the cost, to fight and not to heed the wounds, to toil and not to seek for rest, to labour and not to ask for any reward save that of knowing that we do thy will.

IGNATIUS LOYOLA

O God, help me to go on at all times, when I would like to stop.

Help me, when I feel discouraged because things are so difficult, to keep on until I overcome the difficulties.

Help me, when I get fed up because things are so boring, to remember that I am laying the foundations on which my life will be built.

Help me, when I am driven almost to despair, and when I lose hope of being and doing what I want to be and do, to be ready to lose everything but hope.

Help me to remember that Jesus said that it is he who endures to the end who will be saved, and help me to keep going until I reach my goal;

through Jesus Christ my Lord. Amen.


LOVE'S EXTRAVAGANCE

When Jesus was in Bethany as the guest of Simon the leper, a woman came up to him with an alabaster phial of very expensive perfume, which she poured over his head as he sat at table. The sight of her action annoyed the disciples. 'What is the point of this waste?' they said. 'This could have been sold for a large sum of money, and the proceeds could have been used to help the poor.' Jesus knew what they were saying. 'Why are you distressing the woman?' he said. 'She has done a lovely thing to me. You have the poor with you always, but you do not have me always. By pouring this perfume over my body, she has by her action prepared me for my burial. I tell you truly, wherever this Good News is proclaimed all over the world, what she has done will be told too, so that she will always be remembered.'

Matthew 26:6–13

O Lord our God, grant us grace to desire thee with our whole heart; that, so desiring, we may seek, and seeking find thee; and so finding thee may love thee; and loving thee, may hate those sins from which thou hast redeemed us.

ST ANSELM

O God, give me the things which will make me a good member of the community in which I live.

Give me the forgiving spirit, that I may forgive others, as I hope that you will forgive me.

Give me the tolerant spirit that I may be quicker to praise than to criticize, and that I may be more eager to understand than to condemn.

Give me the unselfish spirit, that I may think even more about the rights of others than about my own rights.

Teach me what to remember and what to forget; to forget all insults and injuries, and to remember all that has been done for me by other people.

Help me always to aim at putting more into life than I take out of it:

through Jesus Christ my Lord. Amen.

### THE LAST SUPPER

When evening came, Jesus took his place at the table with his twelve disciples. During the meal he said to them: 'I tell you truly, one of you will betray me.' They were very distressed, and each of them said to him: 'Master, surely it can't be me?' Jesus answered: 'It is one who has dipped his bread with me in the dish who is going to betray me. The Son of Man goes out on the road the scripture says he must go. But tragic is the fate of the man by whom the Son of Man is betrayed! It would have been better for that man, if he had never been born!' Judas, who was busy trying to betray him, said: 'Master, surely it can't be me?' Jesus said to him: 'You have said it yourself!'

During the meal Jesus took a loaf. He said the blessing over it, and broke it into pieces, and gave it to his disciples. 'Take! Eat!' he said. 'This means my body.' He took a cup, and gave thanks to God. He gave it to them and said: 'All of you drink it. This means my life-blood, through which the new relationship between man and God is made possible, the blood which is being shed for many, that their sins may be forgiven. I tell you, I shall not drink of this fruit of the vine, until the time comes when I drink it new with you in my Father's kingdom.'

Matthew 26:20–29

Thou, O Lord, who commandest us to ask, grant that we may receive. Thou hast put us upon seeking, let us be happy in finding; thou hast bidden us knock, we pray thee open to us. Be graciously pleased to direct and govern all our thoughts and actions, that for the future we may serve thee, and entirely devote ourselves to obeying thee. Accept us, we beseech thee, and draw us to thyself, that we may henceforth be thine by obedience and love, who are already all thine own as thy creatures – even thine, O Lord, who livest and reignest for ever and ever. Amen.

ST AUGUSTINE

O God, grant me in my life the basic virtues on which alone life can be built:

Courage, always to do what is right, no matter what the consequences;
Fidelity, always to be true to those who trust me;
Justice, that I may give every man his due;
Self-control, that I may be so completely in command of myself, that I may be fit always to serve others;
Charity, that I may live in love to all:

through Jesus Christ my Lord. Amen.

GETHSEMANE

Then Jesus went with them to a place called Gethsemane. 'Sit here while I go over there and pray,' he said to his disciples. He took with him Peter and Zebedee's two sons, and he began to be distressed and distraught in mind. 'My soul is grief-stricken with a grief like death,' he said to them. 'Wait here and share my vigil.' He went a little farther, and flung himself face down on the ground in prayer. 'My Father,' he said, 'if it is possible, don't let this bitter ordeal come to me. But not what I will, but what you will.' He came to his disciples and found them sleeping. He said to Peter: 'So the three of you could not keep vigil with me for one hour? Sleeplessly watch and pray, for you may well all have to face your ordeal of temptation. I know that you mean well and that you want to do the right thing, but human nature is frail.' He went away a second time and prayed again. 'My Father,' he said, 'if there is no escape from this situation, unless I go through it to the bitter end, your will be done.' He came back again, and again he found them sleeping, for they could not keep their eyes open.

Again he went away and left them, and again a third time he prayed the same prayer. Then he came to his disciples and said to them: 'Are you still lying there sleeping? The hour has come for the Son of Man to be delivered into the hands of sinful men. Up! On your way! The traitor is coming!'

Matthew 26:36-46

O Lord Jesu, our only health and our everlasting life, I give myself wholly unto thy will: being sure that the thing cannot perish which is committed unto thy mercy.

Thou, merciful Lord, wast born for my sake: thou didst suffer both hunger and thirst for my sake; thou didst preach and teach, didst pray and fast, for my sake: and finally thou gavest thy most precious body to die and thy blood to be shed on the cross, for my sake. Most merciful Saviour, let all these things profit me which thou freely hast given me. O Lord, into thy hands I commit my soul.

Primer of 1559

O God, I do not know what will happen to me today. Whatever comes, help me to meet it well.

If I have difficult things to do today, help me to keep on trying until they are done.

If I will be tempted to do the wrong things, help me to resist temptation and to do the right.

If things will go well with me, and I have good success, save me from all pride and keep me in humility.

If I have to encounter failure, save me from despair, and help me to try again in hope.

If I am hurt or injured in body or in spirit, keep me from anger and from the desire for revenge and give me the forgiving spirit.

Give me your presence with me all through today, whatever light may shine or shadow fall:

through Jesus Christ my Lord. Amen.

### JESUS ON TRIAL

Those who had arrested Jesus took him to the house of Caiaphas the High Priest, where the experts in the Law and the elders had assembled. Peter followed him at a distance, right into the courtyard of the High Priest's house. He went in and sat down with the attendants to see the end.

The chief priests and the whole Sanhedrin made repeated attempts to find fabricated evidence against Jesus, which could be used to justify them in putting him to death. Many witnesses who were prepared to perjure themselves came forward, but the court was unable to find any evidence upon which it could legitimately proceed. At last two witnesses came forward and said: 'This man said: "I can demolish God's Temple, and in three days I can rebuild it."'

The High Priest stood up and said to Jesus: 'Have you no answer to these allegations which these witnesses are making against you?' Jesus remained silent. The High Priest said to him: 'I call on you to tell us on oath, in the name of the living God – are you the Messiah, the Son of God?' 'If you like to say so,' Jesus said. 'But I tell you, from now on you will see the Son of Man sitting at the right hand of Almighty God, and coming on the clouds of heaven.' At that the High Priest ripped his clothes in horror. 'This statement is blasphemy,' he said. 'What further witnesses do we need? You have actually here and now heard his blasphemous claim. What is your verdict?' They answered: 'He is guilty of a crime for which the penalty is death.' Then they spat in his face, and punched him with their clenched fists. Some of them slapped him across the face. 'Prophesy to us, Messiah,' they said. 'Who struck you?'

Matthew 26:57–68

Guide us, teach us, and strengthen us, O Lord, we beseech thee, until we become such as thou wouldst have us be: pure, gentle, truthful, high-minded, courteous, generous, able, dutiful and useful; for thy honour and glory. Amen.

CHARLES KINGSLEY

# FRIDAY: SIXTH WEEK

O God, give me the gift of self-control.

Give me control of my words that I may never say things of which afterwards I would be ashamed, or for which I would be sorry.

Give me control of my temper, that I may never be swept away by anger.

Give me control of my impulses and passions, that I may have everything under perfect control.

Lord Jesus, take me and control me so that all my deeds and words and thoughts may be in captivity to your obedience. This I ask for your love's sake. Amen.

### THE COLLAPSE OF LOYALTY

Peter was sitting outside in the courtyard. One of the maid-servants came up to him. 'You too were with Jesus the Galilean,' she said. He denied it in front of them all. 'I have no idea what you're talking about,' he said. He went out to the gateway. Another maidservant saw him. She said to the people there: 'This man was with Jesus the Nazarene.' Again he denied it. 'I swear I do not know the man,' he said. Shortly afterwards the bystanders came up to Peter and said to him: 'You certainly are one of them. Indeed you are. Your Galilean accent makes it obvious.' Peter swore he was telling the truth, and called down curses on himself if he was not. 'I do not know the man,' he said. Just then the cock crew, and Peter remembered how Jesus had said: 'Before the cock crows, you will disown me three times.' And he went out and wept bitterly.

Matthew 26:69–75

Give us, O Lord, a mind after thine own heart, that we may delight to do thy will, O our God; and let thy Law be written on our hearts. Give us courage and resolution to do our duty, and a heart to be spent in thy service, and in doing all the good that possibly we can the few remaining days of our pilgrimage here on earth. Grant this, we humbly beseech thee for the sake of Jesus Christ thy son our Lord. Amen.

ARCHBISHOP JOHN TILLOTSON

O God, I look back on this week now as it comes to an end.

> Forgive me for the things which I blush to remember. If
> I have hurt others; if I have failed my friends; if I have
> disappointed those who love me; Lord God, forgive.
> I thank you for all the good things which happened to me
> this week. For any kindness I have received; for any
> word of thanks or praise that I never expected; for any
> success that I have had; thank you, my Father.
> Bless everyone who has been kind to me and who has
> helped me this week; and bless anyone who injured
> me or hurt me, and make me able to forgive.
> Help me to learn the lesson life is meant to teach me, and
> not to make the same mistakes over and over again,
> and so help me to be better in the days that lie ahead;

> through Jesus Christ my Lord. Amen.

**THE CROSS**

From twelve o'clock midday until three o'clock in the afternoon there was darkness over the whole land. About three
o'clock in the afternoon Jesus gave a great shout: 'Eli, Eli,
lama sabachthani?' which means: 'My God, my God, why
have you abandoned me?' When some of the bystanders
heard this, they said: 'He is calling Elijah!' One of them at
once ran and took a sponge and soaked it in vinegar and
put it on a cane, and offered it to him to drink. The others
said: 'Wait! Let us see if Elijah is coming to save him.'
Jesus again shouted at the top of his voice, and died.

The curtain of the Temple which veiled the Holy of
Holies was ripped from top to bottom, and the ground was
shaken and the rocks were split. The tombs were burst
open, and the bodies of many of the people of God who slept

in death were raised to life. They came out of their tombs, and after his resurrection they went into the holy city, and appeared to many. When the company commander and his men who were watching Jesus saw the earthquake and the things which were happening, they were awe-stricken. 'Beyond a doubt,' they said, 'this man was indeed a son of God.'

Matthew 27:45–54

O Lord Jesus Christ, give us grace, we beseech thee, this day to do all we have to do in thy name. May we live as those who bear thy holy name, and solely to the glory of thy name. May we refer all things solely to thee, and receive all from thee. Be thou the beginning and the end of all, the pattern whom we are to copy, the redeemer in whom is our strength, the master whom we are to serve, the friend to whom we may look for comfort and sympathy. May we fix our eyes on thee as our help, our aim, the centre of our being, our everlasting friend. O thou who hast so looked on us that we may see thee, set thine eyes upon us, we beseech thee; steady our unsteadfastness, unite us to thyself, and guide us in whatever path thou seest fit to lead us, till of thine infinite mercy thou wilt bring us to thine eternal presence; for thine own name's sake we ask it. Amen.

CANON EDWARD PUSEY

Help me, O God, to use this, your day, to improve myself in every way.

Help me to take the physical exercise which will improve my physical fitness.

Help me to read some good book or to listen to some wise teacher to improve my mental fitness.

Help me to think about Jesus, and in my mind's eye to see him going about doing good, so that his love for all men may increase within my heart.

And help me today to do something for someone who needs my help, so that the love within my heart may turn to deeds;

through Jesus Christ my Lord. Amen.

**THE RISEN CHRIST**

Late on the Sabbath, just as the day was breaking on the Sunday, Mary from Magdala and the other Mary came to look at the tomb. There was a great earthquake, for the angel of the Lord came down from heaven, and came and rolled away the stone, and sat on it. His face shone like lightning, and his clothes were as white as snow. The guards were shaken with fear, and lay like dead men. The angel said to the women: 'Do not be afraid. I know that you are looking for Jesus who was crucified. He is not here, for he has risen, as he said he would. Come! See for yourselves the place where his body lay. Hurry and tell his disciples that he has risen from the dead, and that he is going on ahead of you into Galilee. You will meet him there. That is the message I have for you.' They hurried away from the tomb in mingled awe and great joy, and ran to tell the news to the disciples. Suddenly Jesus was standing in their path. 'Joy be with you,' he said. They went up to him, and clasped his feet, and knelt before him. Then Jesus said to them: 'Don't be afraid. Go and tell my brothers to leave for Galilee. They will see me there.'

Matthew 28:1–10

Give us, O Lord, purity of lips, clean and innocent hearts, and rectitude of action; give us humility, patience, self-wisdom and understanding, the spirit of counsel and strength, the spirit of knowledge and godliness, and of thy fear; make us ever to seek thy face with all our heart, all our soul, all our mind; grant us to have a contrite and humbled heart in thy presence, to prefer nothing to thy love. Have mercy upon us, we humbly beseech thee; through Jesus our Lord. Amen.

Gallican Sacramentary

# CHRISTMAS

O God, on this Christmas Day, I thank you for Jesus.

I thank you that he took our ordinary life upon himself.

I thank you that he was born not in a palace but in a stable.

I thank you that it was not earthly wealth and ease that he knew, but that he was born into a humble home, where he had to work for a living.

I thank you that he had to grow up and to learn as any boy must, and that he was obedient to his parents as any boy must be.

Help me to be like him, and grant that on this Christmas Day I may think more of giving than of getting.

I thank you for a happy home. Grant that I may show my gratitude for all your gifts by living more like him who was born in Bethlehem on the first Christmas Day.

This I ask for your love's sake. Amen.

### THE WORD BECAME FLESH

When the world began, the Word was already there. The Word was with God, and the nature of the Word was the same as the nature of God. The Word was there in the beginning with God. It was through the agency of the Word that everything else came into being. Without the Word not one single thing came into being. As for the whole creation, the Word was the life principle in it, and that life was the light of men. The light continues to shine in the darkness, and the darkness has never extinguished it.

On to the stage of history there came a man sent from God. His name was John. The purpose of his coming was to declare the truth, and the truth he declared was about the light. The aim of his declaration was to persuade all men to believe. He himself was not the light. His only function was to tell men about the light. The real light, the light which enlightens every man, was just about to come into the world. He was in the world, and, although it was through him that the world came into being, the world failed to recognize him. It was to his own home that he came, but his own people refused to receive him. But to all who did receive him he gave the privilege of becoming God's children. That privilege was given to those who do believe that he really is what he is. They were born, not by the common processes of physical birth, not as the consequence of some moment of sexual passion, not as a result of any man's desire. Their birth came from God.

John 1:1-13

Moonless darkness stands between,
Past, O Past, no more be seen!
But the Bethlehem star may lead me
To the sight of him who freed me
From the self that I have been.
Make me pure, Lord: thou art holy;
Make me meek, Lord: thou wert lowly;
Now beginning, and alway:
Now begin, on Christmas day.

GERARD MANLEY HOPKINS

# NEW YEAR'S DAY

O God, you can make all things new.

I thank you for this New Year, and for the chance to
begin again.
Help me this year to be kinder and more considerate than
I have been up to now.
Help me to work and study harder than ever I did before.
Help me to conquer the temptations which will attack me.
Help me all through this year to aim high and to reach
my target;

through Jesus Christ my Lord. Amen.


FROM EVERLASTING TO EVERLASTING

Lord, thou hast been our dwelling place
in all generations.
Before the mountains were brought forth,
or ever thou hadst formed the earth and the world,
from everlasting to everlasting thou art God.

Thou turnest man back to the dust, and sayest, 'Turn
back, O children of men!'
For a thousand years in thy sight are but as yesterday
when it is past, or as a watch in the night.

Let thy work be manifest to thy servants,
and thy glorious power to their children.
Let the favour of the Lord our God be upon us,
and establish thou the work of our hands upon us,
yea, the work of our hands establish thou it.

Psalm 90:1–4, 16–17

# NEW YEAR'S DAY

Eternal God, who makest all things new, and abidest for ever the same: Grant us to begin this year in thy faith, and to continue it in thy favour; that, guided in all our doings, and guarded all our days, we may spend our lives in thy service, and finally, by thy grace, attain the glory of everlasting life; through Jesus Christ our Lord.

Order of Divine Service for Public Worship

# GOOD FRIDAY

Lord Jesus, help me to remember that on this day you were crucified for us.

And grant that as I remember your love and your suffering I may be lost in wonder, love and praise, and that I may come to love you as you first loved me.

For your love's sake I ask it. Amen.

### THE CROSS

One of the criminals who had been crucified kept hurling insults at Jesus. 'Are you not the Messiah?' he said. 'Save yourself and us!' The other sternly reprimanded him. 'Have you no reverence for God?' he said. 'You have been sentenced to the same punishment as he has been, and we with justice, for we are getting what we deserve for our misdeeds, but he has committed no crime. Jesus,' he said, 'remember me when you come into your Kingdom.' Jesus said to him: 'Very certainly you will be with me in Paradise today.'

By this time it was about twelve o'clock midday, and darkness came over the whole land until three o'clock in the afternoon, for the sun was in eclipse. The curtain of the Temple which veiled the Holy of Holies was ripped down the middle. Jesus shouted at the top of his voice. Then he said: 'Father, into your hands I entrust my spirit.' When he had said this, he died.

Luke 23:39–46

# GOOD FRIDAY

O blessed Saviour, draw us; draw us by the cords of thy
love; draw us by the sense of thy goodness; draw us by
thyself; draw us by the unspotted purity and beauty of thy
example; draw us by the merit of thy precious death and
by the power of thy Holy Spirit; draw us, good Lord, and
we shall run after thee. Amen.

THE REV DR ISAAC BARROW

Lord Jesus, I thank you that on the first Easter Day you
conquered death and the grave and rose to life again.

I thank you that you are not only a memory, but that you
are also a living presence.

I thank you that you promised to be with us to the end of
the world and beyond.

Help me to remember that all life is lived in your unseen
presence, and help me to make it fit for you to see.

This I ask for your love's sake. Amen.


## THE GREAT RECOGNITION

On Sunday Mary from Magdala went to the tomb so early
in the morning that it was still dark. When she saw that the
stone had been removed from the tomb, she went running
to Simon Peter and to the other disciple, the disciple who
was specially dear to Jesus. 'They have taken away the
Master from the tomb,' she said, 'and we don't know where
they have put him.' Peter and the other disciple set out on
the way to the tomb. They both began to run. The other
disciple ran on ahead, faster than Peter, and reached the
tomb first. He stooped down and looked in, and saw the
linen grave-clothes lying there, but he did not go in. Simon
Peter arrived after him, and went into the tomb. He saw the
linen grave-clothes lying there, and he saw the towel, which
had been round Jesus' head, lying not with the other
grave-clothes, but still in its folds, separately in a place
all by itself. Then the other disciple, who had arrived
at the tomb first, went in, and when he saw the inside
of the tomb he was convinced. As yet they did not understand that scripture said that Jesus had to rise from the
dead. So the disciples went back home.

John 20:1–10

O merciful God, the Father of our Lord Jesus Christ, who is the resurrection and the life; in whom whosoever believeth shall live, though he die; and whosoever liveth and believeth in him shall not die eternally. We bless thy holy name for all thy servants departed in this life in thy faith and fear; beseeching thee to give us grace so to follow their good example that with them we may be partakers of thy heavenly kingdom. Grant this, O Father, for Jesus Christ's sake, our only advocate and redeemer. Amen.

Sarum Missal

God, grant to me also the help of your Holy Spirit.

Let your Holy Spirit guide my thinking so that all my
thoughts may be clean, and so that I may reach a
solution to all the problems which perplex me.
Let your Holy Spirit guide my footsteps, so that I may
never lose the way or take the wrong way.
Let your Holy Spirit control my tongue so that I may
never speak a word which is untrue, unclean or unkind.
Let your Holy Spirit guide and direct my whole life so
that I may keep to the straight pathway until my
journey's end;
through Jesus Christ my Lord. Amen.

#### THE COMING OF THE SPIRIT

The disciples were all passing the day of Pentecost together.
All of a sudden a sound came from the sky like a blast of
violent wind, and it filled the whole house where they were
sitting. There appeared to them what looked like tongues of
fire, which divided themselves up, and settled on each one
of them. They were all filled with the Holy Spirit, and began
to speak in other languages, as the Spirit enabled them to
speak.

There were Jews staying in Jerusalem, devout men who
had come from every nation under the sun. When they
heard the sound of this, they came in their crowds. They
were bewildered, because each of them was hearing the
disciples speaking in his own language. They were astonished and amazed. 'Aren't all these men who are speaking
Galileans?' they said. 'How then is it that each one of us
hears them speaking in the language we have spoken since
we were born? Parthians and Medes and Elamites, those
whose homes are in Mesopotamia, Judaea and Cappadocia,

Pontus and Asia, Phrygia and Pamphylia, Egypt and the Cyrenian parts of Libya, visitors from Rome, Jews and converts to Judaism, Cretans and Arabians, we are hearing them telling of God's great deeds in our own languages.' They were all astonished, and completely at a loss what to make of it. 'What is the meaning of this?' they said to each other. Others treated the whole affair as a jest. 'They are full of new wine,' they said.

Acts 2:1–13

God, who as at this time didst teach the hearts of thy faithful people by sending to them the light of thy Holy Spirit, grant us by the same Spirit to have a right judgement in all things and evermore to rejoice in his holy comfort; through the merits of Christ Jesus our saviour, who liveth and reigneth with thee in the unity of the same Spirit, one God, world without end. Amen.

Gregorian Sacramentary

# FIRST DAY OF TERM

O God, today is for me the first day of a new term.

I thank you for everyone who has taught me and for all that
I have learned up to now.
Help me to use this new term wisely and to use it well.
Help me to use to the full the opportunities of learning
which will come to me.
Help me to count as a day wasted when I do not learn
something new.

All through this term help me to be friendly towards my
fellow-pupils and respectful towards my teachers.
Help me to work hard and to play hard, so that I may be a
good citizen of my school, through Jesus Christ my Lord.
Amen.

## THE EXCELLENT THINGS

Never lose your Christian joy. Let me say it again! Never
lose it! You must make it common knowledge that you
never insist on the letter of the law. It will not be long now
until the Lord comes. Don't worry about anything. In
every circumstance of life tell God about the things you
want to ask him for in your prayers and your requests to
him, and bring him your thanks too. And God's peace,
which is beyond both our understanding and our con-
triving, will stand guard over your hearts and minds,
because your life is linked for ever with the life of Christ
Jesus.

It only remains to say, brothers, that your thoughts must
continually dwell on everything that is true, on everything
that is nobly serious, on everything that is right, on everything that is pure, on everything that is lovely, on everything that is honourable, on all that men call excellence,

and on all that wins men's praise. You must keep putting into practice the lessons you have learned from me, the instructions you have received from me, and the example I have given you in speech and in action. And then the God of peace will be with you.

Philippians 4:4–9

O God of time and eternity, who makest us creatures of time, to the end that when time is over we may attain to thy blessed eternity. With time, which is thy gift, give us also wisdom to redeem the time lest our day of grace be lost, for the sake of Christ Jesus our Lord. Amen.

C. G. ROSSETTI

# EXAMINATION TIME

O God, give me your help at this examination time.
Keep me from being nervous and keep me calm, so that I
will be able to do my best.
If I am not prepared, I have no excuse. If I am prepared,
and if I have done my best, give me the calm and the
freedom from nerves I need to do well;
through Jesus Christ my Lord. Amen.


## THE YOKE IN YOUTH

The steadfast love of the Lord never ceases,
his mercies never come to an end;
they are new every morning;
great is thy faithfulness.
'The Lord is my portion,' says my soul,
'therefore I will hope in him.'

The Lord is good to those who wait for him,
to the soul that seeks him.
It is good that one should wait quietly
for the salvation of the Lord.
It is good for a man that he bear the
yoke in his youth.

Lamentations 3:22–27

# EXAMINATION TIME

O God, the sovereign good of the soul, who requirest the hearts of all thy children, deliver us from all sloth in thy work, all coldness in thy cause; and grant us by looking unto thee to rekindle our love, and by waiting upon thee to renew our strength; through Jesus Christ our Lord. Amen.

WILLIAM BRIGHT

# THE DAY OF THE MATCH

O God, I thank you that you have made me strong enough
in limb and fit enough in body to play in this match
today.

Help me to play hard but to play fair. Make me such that I
would rather lose the match than win by unfair or foul
means.

If we win keep me from boasting about it, and if we lose
keep me from making excuses; through Jesus Christ my
Lord. Amen.

## PRESSING TO THE GOAL

Beware of these dogs! Beware of these manufacturers of
wickedness! Beware of those whose circumcision is no
better than mutilation! It is we who are really circumcised,
for we offer God a worship directed by his Spirit. Our
pride is in Christ Jesus. We place no reliance on human
externals, although I might well base my claims on such
things. If anyone thinks that he can rely on physical marks
and human achievements, I have an even stronger claim.
I was circumcised on the eighth day after I was born. I am
a pure-blooded Israelite. I belong to the tribe of Benjamin.
I am a Hebrew and the son of Hebrew parents. In my
attitude to the Jewish law I was a Pharisee. So enthusiastic
was my devotion to the law that I was a persecutor of the
church. As far as the goodness which the law prescribes and
demands is concerned, I was beyond criticism. But whatever achievements in my life and career I would once have
reckoned among the profits of life, I have written off as a
dead loss for the sake of Christ. Yes, and more than that – I
am prepared to write off everything as a dead loss for the
sake of getting to know Christ Jesus my Lord, for that
knowledge is something which surpasses everything in the
world. For his sake I have abandoned everything, and I
regard all else as of no more value than filth for the garbage
heap. For me the only thing of value in the world is to gain
Christ, and to make my life one with his. I am not right with

God through any legalistic achievement of my own. All I want is the relationship with God which only God himself can give me, all founded on faith in Christ. My one aim is to know Christ, and to experience the power of his resurrection, and to share with him in his sufferings. My aim is to die the death he died, so that, if it may be, I may reach the resurrection from the dead.

I do not claim that I have already attained this, or that I have already reached perfection. I press on to try to grasp that for which Christ Jesus has already grasped me. Brothers, I do not regard myself as having already grasped the prize. But I have one aim in life – to forget what lies behind, and to strain every nerve to reach what lies ahead. And so I press on to the goal to win the prize to which God in Christ Jesus calls me upward and onward.

Philippians 3:2-14

Grant that we may walk as Christ walked; Grant that what the Spirit was in him, such he may be also in us; Grant that our lives may be refashioned after the pattern of his life; Grant that we may do today here on earth what Christ would have done, and in the way he would have done it; Grant that we may become vessels of his grace, instruments of his will – to thy honour and glory; through Jesus Christ our Lord. Amen.

J. H. JOWETT

O God, thank you for bringing me to the end of another term.

Forgive me for the time I have wasted, and for the opportunities I have missed.

Thank you for all that I have learned during this term, and thank you for any new friends I have made and all the old friends I have kept.

Thank you for those who encouraged me when I was feeling discouraged, and thank you for those who had patience with me when I was very annoying.

Help me to remember all that I have been taught, so that when I come back next term I may make even better progress;

through Jesus Christ my Lord. Amen.

## THE ARMOUR OF THE SPIRIT

Finally, your union with the Lord and with his mighty power must give you a dynamic strength. Put on the complete armour which God can give you, and then you will be able to resist the stratagems of the Devil. For our struggle is not against any human foe; it is against demonic rulers and authorities, against the cosmic powers of this dark world, against spiritual forces of evil in the heavens. So then, take the complete armour which God can give you, and then, when the evil day comes, you will be able to see things through to the end, and to remain erect. So then take your stand. Buckle the belt of truth round your waist. Put on righteousness for a breastplate. Put preparedness to preach the gospel of peace on your feet like shoes. Through thick and thin take faith as your shield. With it you will be able to extinguish all the flaming arrows of the Evil One. Take salvation as your helmet. Take the sword the Spirit gives. That sword is the word of God. Keep on praying fervently, and asking God for what you need, and on every occasion let the Spirit be the atmosphere in which you pray. To that end sleeplessly and always persevere in your requests to God for all God's consecrated people. Pray for me too, and ask God to give me a message when I have to speak. Pray that I may be able fearlessly to tell men the secret of the good news, for which I am an ambassador, though now in chains. I need your prayers to enable me to speak it with the fearlessness with which I ought to speak.

Ephesians 6:10–20

Grant, O Lord, that what we have said with our lips, we may believe in our hearts and practise in our lives; and of thy mercy keep us faithful unto the end; for Christ's sake. Amen.

JOHN HUNTER

# GOING TO WORK FOR THE FIRST TIME

O God, bless me as I go out to work for the first time.
In my work help me always to do my best, so that I may be
a workman who never has any need to be ashamed.
Help me to work equally hard whether I am watched or
not, always remembering that you see me, and always
trying to make my work good enough to offer to you.
Help me always to remember that Jesus worked in the
carpenter's shop in Nazareth, and help me to be as good
a workman as he was.
This I ask for your love's sake. Amen.


A GOOD WORKMAN

Remember Jesus Christ, risen from the dead, descended
from David. This is what my gospel teaches. It is for the
sake of that gospel that I am at present suffering, even to
the length of being imprisoned as a criminal. But no
one can put the word of God in prison. It is for the sake of
God's chosen ones that I can pass the breaking-point and
not break. I want them too to win that salvation which is
ours because of what Christ Jesus has done for us, and with
it the glory that is eternal. It has been said, and said truly:

> If we have died with him,
>     we shall live with him;
> if we endure,
>     we shall reign with him;
> if we deny him,
>     he too will deny us;
> if we are faithless,
>     he remains faithful,
>         for he cannot deny himself.

Keep on reminding them of all this. Charge them before God not to engage in pugnacious debates about verbal niceties. Debates like that are an unprofitable occupation, and do nothing but undermine the faith of the hearers. Do your best to present yourself to God as a man of sterling worth, a workman who has no need to be ashamed of his work, a sound expositor of the true word.

*2 Timothy 2:8–15*

Do thou thyself, O Lord, send out thy light and thy truth, and enlighten the eyes of our minds to understand thy divine Word. Give us grace to be hearers of it, and not hearers only, but doers of the Word, that we may bring forth good fruit abundantly and be counted worthy of the kingdom of heaven. And to thee, O Lord our God, we ascribe glory and thanksgiving, now and for ever. Amen.

*Liturgy of the Greek Church*

# FOR FRIENDS

I thank you for my friends, for those who understand me better than I understand myself, for those who know me at my worst and still like me, for those who have forgiven me when I had no right to expect to be forgiven.

Help me to be as true to my friends as I would wish them to be to me.

Help me to take the first step to get into touch again with friends from whom I have drifted apart.

And help me to have no bitterness but only forgiveness to any of my friends who failed or who turned against me; through Jesus Christ my Lord. Amen.


TRUE FRIENDSHIP

Then they lifted up their voices and wept again; and Orpah kissed her mother-in-law, but Ruth clung to her.

And she said, 'See, your sister-in-law has gone back to her people and to her gods; return after your sister-in-law.' But Ruth said, 'Entreat me not to leave you or to return from following you; for where you go I will go, and where you lodge I will lodge; your people shall be my people, and your God my God; where you die I will die, and there will I be buried. May the Lord do so to me and more also if even death parts me from you.' And when Naomi saw that she was determined to go with her, she said no more.

Ruth 1:14–18

# FOR FRIENDS

May thy Spirit hallow, and thy Grace fortify, O blessed Lord, friends and others for whom we would seek thine aid: those of closest tie, those of greatest need.

May thy divine power protect and provide for them. May thy peace comfort them. May thy pardon reassure them, and thy precious blood redeem them. May thy prosperity attend them. May daily progress be theirs in the heavenly way; through Christ Jesus our Lord. Amen.

A Chain of Prayer Across the Ages

# IN THE TIME OF ILLNESS

O God, bless me in this illness that has come to me.
Make me a good patient, always obedient to the doctor's
  instructions, always cheerful and always uncomplaining.
I remember before you all other people who are ill and in
  pain. Help them and help me to get better soon.
Thank you for all the people who look after me so well,
  and for all that they do for me.
Help me to show my gratitude by never grumbling or
  complaining, and by being cheerful even when being
  cheerful is difficult; through Jesus Christ my Lord.
  Amen.

### GOD'S DELIVERANCE

I love the Lord, because he has heard
  my voice and my supplications.
Because he inclined his ear to me,
  therefore I will call on him as long as I live.
The snares of death encompassed me;
  the pangs of Sheol laid hold on me;
  I suffered distress and anguish.
Then I called on the name of the Lord:
  'O Lord, I beseech thee, save my life!'

Gracious is the Lord, and righteous;
  our God is merciful.
The Lord preserves the simple;
  when I was brought low, he saved me.
Return, O my soul, to your rest;
  for the Lord has dealt bountifully with you.

For thou hast delivered my soul from death,
  my eyes from tears,
  my feet from stumbling.

Psalm 116:1–8

# IN THE TIME OF ILLNESS

O Lord, forasmuch as it is an easy thing with thee to give life to the dead, restore, we pray thee, to the sick their former health, and grant that they who seek the healing of thy heavenly mercy, may also obtain the remedies necessary for the body; through Jesus Christ our Lord. Amen.

Gothic Missal

# IN DISAPPOINTMENT

O God, you know me better than I know myself, and you know how disappointed I have been at this time.

The thing that I had set my heart on was not for me. The friends I trusted proved untrue.
I honestly tried so hard, and I failed.

Help me, O God, to accept things as they are. Help me not to waste my time on vain regrets and unhappy memories. Help me to begin again and to try again. Help me always to look forward and not back. Help me to forget the things that are behind and ever to press forward to the things which are ahead; through Jesus Christ my Lord. Amen.

## WHY ARE YOU CAST DOWN?

Oh send out thy light and thy truth;
   let them lead me,
let them bring me to thy holy hill
   and to thy dwelling!
Then I will go to the altar of God,
   to God my exceeding joy;
and I will praise thee with the lyre,
   O God, my God.

Why are you cast down, O my soul,
   and why are you disquieted within me?
Hope in God; for I shall again praise him,
   my help and my God.

Psalm 43:3–5

# IN DISAPPOINTMENT

Stretch forth, O Lord, thy mercy over all thy servants everywhere, even the right hand of heavenly help, that they may seek thee with their whole heart, and obtain what they rightly ask for; through Jesus Christ our Lord. Amen.

Gelasian Sacramentary

# IN SUCCESS

O God, I thank you that I have done well. I thank you for success.

Keep me from being conceited; keep me humble.

Help me to remember all those to whom I owe my success, those who taught me and trained me, and who encouraged me when I was tired and depressed.

Help me not to sit back and admire myself, but help me to see that, whatever I have achieved there are still higher heights to climb, and still further goals to reach. Whatever praise I receive, help me always to be my own severest critic; through Jesus Christ my Lord. Amen.

## TRUE GOODNESS

If there is such a thing as Christian encouragement, if there is such a thing as love's comforting power, if you and I are really sharing in the partnership which only the Holy Spirit can make possible, if you really wish to show me a heartfelt sympathy which is like the mercy of God, make my joy complete by being in perfect harmony of mind, by joining in a common love for God and for each other, by sharing in a common life, by taking every decision in unity of mind, by never acting from motives of competitive rivalry or in the conceited desire for empty prestige. If you want to make my joy complete, instead of that each of you must humbly think the other better than himself; each of you must concentrate, not on his own interest, but on the interests of others also. Try always to have the same attitude to life as Jesus had.

# IN SUCCESS

He shared the very being of God,
but he did not regard his equality to God
    as a thing to be clutched to himself.
So far from that, he emptied himself,
    and really and truly became a servant,
and was made for a time exactly like men.
In a human form that all could see,
    he accepted such a depth of humiliation
    that he was prepared to die,
        and to die on a cross.
That is why God has given him the highest place,
    and has conferred on him
    the name that is greater than any name,
so that at the name of Jesus every creature
    in heaven, and on earth, and beneath the earth
should kneel in reverence and submission,
and so that everything which has a voice
    should openly declare
    that Jesus Christ is Lord,
and thus bring glory to God the Father.

*Philippians 2:1-11*

O Lord, give us more charity, more self-denial, more likeness to thee. Teach us to sacrifice our comforts to others, and our likings for the sake of doing good. Teach us that it is better to give than to receive, better to forget ourselves than to put ourselves forward; better to minister than to be ministered unto. And unto thee, the God of love, be all glory and praise, both now and for ever more. Amen.

HENRY ALFORD

O God, today another year of life is finished and another year of life has begun.

Thank you for bringing me safely through another year.

Grant that I may not only be a year older, but also a year wiser.

Help me to profit by experience, so that I may not make the same mistakes over and over again.

O God, at the end of one year of life and at the beginning of another, I cannot help remembering all that I meant to do and to be in the year that is just past, and how little I have actually done. Help me in this incoming year really to carry out my resolutions and intentions, so that when I come to the end of it there may be no regrets; through Jesus Christ my Lord. Amen.

## THE PASSING YEARS

Lord, thou hast been our dwelling place
  in all generations.
Before the mountains were brought forth,
  or ever thou hadst formed the earth and the world,
  from everlasting to everlasting thou art God.

Thou turnest man back to the dust,
  and sayest, 'Turn back, O children of men!'
For a thousand years in thy sight
  are but as yesterday when it is past,
  or as a watch in the night.

Thou dost sweep men away; they are like a dream,
  like grass which is renewed in the morning:
in the morning it flourishes and is renewed;
  in the evening it fades and withers.

# FOR A BIRTHDAY

For we are consumed by thy anger;
  by thy wrath we are overwhelmed.
Thou hast set our iniquities before thee,
  our secret sins in the light of thy countenance.

For all our days pass away under thy wrath,
  our years come to an end like a sigh.
The years of our life are threescore and ten,
  or even by reason of strength fourscore;
yet their span is but toil and trouble;
  they are soon gone, and we fly away.

Who considers the power of thy anger,
  and thy wrath according to the fear of thee?
So teach us to number our days
  that we may get a heart of wisdom.

Psalm 90:1–12

It is my birthday, Lord Jesus, my saviour, and I thank thee
for giving me the wonderful gift of life. I pray thee that I
may use my life rightly, that I may try to grow braver,
kinder, wiser and truer year by year. I thank thee for all the
joys of the past year, and pray thee to bless me through the
coming one. Help me to conquer my faults and live more
to thy glory. Grant me thy grace to help all those around me,
and to try and make them happy. Be with me step by step
all through this new year, and keep me safe unto the end;
for thy sake. Amen.

A Chain of Prayer Across the Ages

# AT THE END OF THE YEAR

O God, as this year comes to an end, I think back and
  remember.
I remember the time I have wasted.
I remember the things I meant to do and have not done.
I remember the resolutions I made and broke.
I remember the laziness which resented any effort.
I remember how easily side-tracked I have been.
I have so often been lured away from the things that matter
  by the things which do not matter.
Forgive me for the past and strengthen me for the future,
  and help me so to live this year that at the end of it I may
  have no regrets; through Jesus Christ my Lord. Amen.


THE LAW OF SUCCESS
  Blessed is the man
      who walks not in the counsel of the wicked,
      nor stands in the way of sinners,
          nor sits in the seat of scoffers;
      but his delight is in the law of the Lord,
          and on his law he meditates day and night.
  He is like a tree
      planted by streams of water,
  that yields its fruit in its season,
      and its leaf does not wither.
  In all that he does he prospers.

  The wicked are not so,
      but are like chaff which the wind drives away.
  Therefore the wicked will not stand in the judgement,
      nor sinners in the congregation of the righteous;
  for the Lord knows the way of the righteous,
      but the way of the wicked will perish.

                                              Psalm 1

# AT THE END OF THE YEAR

O Lord, in whose hands are life and death, by whose power I am sustained, and by whose mercy I am spared, look down upon me with pity. Forgive me that I have until now so much neglected the duty which thou hast assigned to me, and suffered the days and hours of which I must give account to pass away without any endeavour to accomplish thy will. Make me to remember, O God, that every day is thy gift and ought to be used according to thy command. Grant me, therefore, so to repent of my negligence, that I may obtain mercy from thee, and pass the time which thou shalt yet allow me in diligent performance of thy commands, through Jesus Christ. Amen.

SAMUEL JOHNSON

# Fount Paperbacks

Fount is one of the leading paperback publishers of religious books and below are some of its recent titles.

☐ PAUL THE INTERPRETER George Appleton  £2.95
☐ ACTING AS FRIENDS Michael De-la-Noy  £4.50
☐ THE BURNING BUSH John Drury  £2.99
☐ A KEY TO THE OLD TESTAMENT
David Edwards  £3.50
☐ THE CRY OF THE SPIRIT Tatiana Goricheva  £3.99
☐ CROSSFIRE Richard Holloway  £3.50
☐ CREATION Martin Israel  £2.99
☐ BEING IN LOVE William Johnston  £3.50
☐ THE MASS J. M. Lustiger  £2.99
☐ CALLED TO HOLINESS Ralph Martin  £2.95
☐ THE HIDDEN JOURNEY Melvyn Matthews  £3.50
☐ REFLECTIONS ON MY WORK Thomas Merton  £3.99
☐ DEATH BE NOT PROUD Peter Mullen  £2.99
☐ SCRIPTURE PROMISES Carmen Rojas  £3.50
☐ LIGHT AND LIFE Grazyna Sikorska  £2.95
☐ EASTER GARDEN Nicola Slee  £3.95
☐ CHRISTMAS – AND ALWAYS Rita Snowden  £2.99
☐ CELEBRATION Margaret Spufford  £2.95

All Fount Paperbacks are available at your bookshop or newsagent, or they can be ordered by post from Fount Paperbacks, Cash Sales Department, G.P.O. Box 29, Douglas, Isle of Man. Please send purchase price plus 22p per book, maximum postage £3. Customers outside the UK send purchase price, plus 22p per book. Cheque, postal order or money order. No currency.

NAME (Block letters) _____

ADDRESS_____

_____

_____